Nehemiah: Man in Charge

Donald K. Campbell

While this book is designed for the reader's personal enjoyment and profit, is is also intended for group study. A Leader's Guide with Victor Multiuse Transparency Masters is available from your local bookstore or from the publisher at $2.25.

VICTOR BOOKS

a division of SP Publications, Inc., Wheaton, Illinois
Offices also in Fullerton, California • Whitby, Ontario, Canada • London, England

Unless otherwise noted, Scripture quotations are taken from the King James Version (KJV). Other quotations are from the *New American Standard Bible* (NASB), © 1960, 1962, 1968, 1971, 1972, 1973 by the Lockman Foundation, La Habra, California; *The Living Bible* (LB), © Tyndale House Publishers, Wheaton, Ill.; *The New Berkeley Version in Modern English* (BERK), © 1945, 1959, 1969 by the Zondervan Publishing House. All quotations used by permission.

Recommended Dewey Decimal Classification: 222.8
Suggested Subject headings: Bible. O.T.—Biography; Bible—History; Leadership

Library of Congress Catalog Card Number: 78-57954
ISBN: 0-88207-781-3

VICTOR BOOKS
A division of SP Publications, Inc.
P.O. Box 1825, Wheaton, Illinois 60187

To my parents
Mr. and Mrs. Dwight Campbell
who rooted me in God's truth
and guided me in God's way
in preparation for my mission in life

Contents

1

The Man Who Got Involved

Catherine Genovese, coming home from her night job early one April morning in 1964, was attacked and repeatedly stabbed. Her cries for help went unheeded, though 38 residents of that New York neighborhood witnessed the attack. The sense of outrage was nationwide and Senator Russell of Georgia even read the *New York Times* account of the crime into the *Congressional Record*.

But the policy of noninvolvement is increasingly a pattern of the present generation. A Christian woman was overheard to say, "I prefer to get lost in a big church." She wanted to sit on the sidelines and avoid any involvement or responsibility.

Nehemiah was different. He recognized the seriousness of a situation and accepted the responsibility for dealing with it.

Nehemiah's Inquiry (1:1-3)

Plunging suddenly into his story, Nehemiah does not give us much of his previous history. We learn that he was the son of Hacaliah and a child of the captivity living in Shushan (the Greeks called it Susa). His residence was the royal palace because he was the king's cupbearer (vv. 1, 11b).

Magnificent ruins of the royal residence at Susa were uncovered by French archeologists between 1880-1890, and enable us to recreate the splendor of Nehemiah's surroundings. The palace was shown to have been built with cedar, gold, silver, and ivory imported from various countries. Artistically colored glazed bricks and relief designs of winged bulls decorated the palace.

Why was a godly man like Nehemiah living in comfort in Persia when thousands of his fellow Jews had returned to Jerusalem with Ezra in 458 B.C.? Since it was now 13 years later (445 B.C., the 20th year of Artaxerxes I), it may be supposed that Nehemiah was either too young to return with that expedition or was already serving at the court in a position he did not feel led to leave at the time.

How important was Nehemiah's position as the king's cup-bearer? Was he not just another palace servant? George Rawlinson, a professor of ancient history, describes the Persian court as splendid and magnificent. The king was surrounded by hundreds of personal attendants, and within the precincts of the palace as many as 15,000 persons were fed daily. The monarch, however, rarely dined with his guests but was normally served alone, and that is where the cupbearer came in:

> The special duty of the cupbearers was to fill the royal winecup from the vase or flagon, which stood on or near the royal board, and to hand it daintily and grace-fully to their august master, supporting it with three fingers, and presenting it in such a way that the king could readily take it from their hand without any danger of spilling a single drop. Before filling the cup they carefully washed it out, and before offering it to their master they ladled out a small quantity with their left hand, and swallowed it, to show that, so far as their knowledge went, it was not poisoned. When not engaged in this, their main duty, they guarded the en-trance to the royal apartment, and allowed persons to enter, or forbade them, at their discretion. Even princes of the blood royal had to submit; and the power, thus practically exercised of allowing or preventing audi-ences, made the office one of high account, and prob-ably enabled its holder, if he were so inclined, to greatly enrich himself (George Rawlinson, *Ezra and Nehemiah —Their Lives and Times* [New York: Fleming H. Revell Company, n.d.], p. 86).

Something occurred one day that was to change Nehemiah's life and work dramatically—he met a group of Persian Jews who had just returned to Susa after a trip to Jerusalem. Josephus, a first-century Jewish historian, suggested that Nehemiah was strolling outside the palace one evening when some travel-stained men passed him on their way into the city, conversing together in the Hebrew tongue. Forgetting all about Artaxerxes' supper, Nehemiah eagerly inquired about the plight of his fellow countrymen who had escaped exile and about Jerusalem itself (v. 2).

The answer he received was disheartening: "The remnant that are left of the captivity there in the province are in great affliction and reproach; the wall of Jerusalem is broken down and the gates thereof are burned with fire" (v. 3). What catastrophe were they referring to? Many scholars assume the state of the city described here had continued from the fall of Jerusalem in 586 B.C. and the destruction of its walls by Nebuchadnezzar at that time. But would the pilgrims have given as the latest news about Jerusalem a description of the condition in which it had stood for a century and a half? And would Nehemiah have been so distressed by a calamity which had taken place 150 years before?

We must assume, therefore, that since 536 B.C. (the return under Zerubbabel), not only had the temple and homes of the people been rebuilt, but some progress had been made toward the rebuilding of the walls and gates (see Ezra 4:7-24). It was the frustration of these recent efforts and the sorry state of Jerusalem that distressed Nehemiah. It had been said that in the ancient world "a city without locked gates and lofty walls was no city at all." Nehemiah, a devoted Jew, wept at the news that Jerusalem, the holy city, was without walls and at the mercy of hostile neighbors and marauding bands of robbers.

One writer has well said, "Nehemiah began his efforts with a listening ear. In contrast with much leadership which begins with the mouth, Nehemiah began his with an ear. He listened" ("Nehemiah and the Peter Principle," A. MacDonald, *Eternity*, October 1974, p. 41).

Nehemiah's Reaction (1:4)

When Nehemiah learned that new disasters had fallen on Jerusalem and the Jewish remnant there, he could have said, "That is too bad, but what can I do about it?" Instead, four vivid verbs in verse 4 tell how the heart of this man was moved because of the sufferings of God's people—he *wept, mourned, fasted,* and *prayed.* Nehemiah did not merely sit down and wring his hands; he did more, much more; through intercessory prayer, he identified himself with the remnant in Judah.

Sadly, many of today's Christians show little concern for the Lord's work while they prosper materially. "The believer who wants his ministry to make a permanent difference must be arrested by a desperate sense of need. One person's concern may be directed toward an aboriginal tribe without the Gospel, while another Christian may be moved to tears by a substandard Christian education program at his local church. Needs come in assorted shapes and sizes, but all of them await the touch of someone with the agony of caring. A burdened God is at work in the world. He searches for burdened believers through whom He may work" ("The Agony of Caring," D. McCarthy, *Sunday School Times and Gospel Herald,* February 1973, p. 15).

Nehemiah's Prayer (1: 5-11)

No doubt the words of Psalm 137:5-6 weighed heavily on the heart of Nehemiah:

> If I forget thee, O Jerusalem,
> let my right hand forget her cunning.
> If I do not remember thee,
> let my tongue cleave to the roof of my mouth;
> if I prefer not Jerusalem
> above my chief joy.

Yet he did not rush immediately into the presence of the king. He knew the importance of spiritual preparation and spent a prolonged period of time in the presence of God. We gain the firm impression from this book that it was a matter of habit with Nehemiah to turn to God in prayer, particularly when he faced problems that were too big to solve.

In a Peanuts comic strip, Lucy has her psychiatric stand all set up, offering a consultation for five cents. Snoopy approaches and sits on the patient's stool but says absolutely nothing. Finally, he simply gets up and leaves. Lucy, frustrated, comments, "Well, what can you do when the patient won't say anything?"

That may be a simple though realistic picture of many believers who go through life attempting to solve their own problems. Nehemiah, however, knew that God had the help he so desperately needed and we find him praying no less than 11 times in the space of these 13 chapters. Certainly, Nehemiah shows us how prayer can be a vital force in our lives.

In many respects the prayer of chapter 1 is a model prayer. It follows the pattern of worship, confession, and petition.

Worship (v. 5). When facing a serious problem, it is helpful to fix our attention on the greatness of God; then the problem shrinks to its real size. Nehemiah, in arresting language, approached God and worshiped Him as the One who is great, awe-inspiring, and faithful.

Nehemiah possessed a clear understanding of the character of God. The writer of an article in a university student newspaper did not exhibit a similar understanding when he variously described God as a venerable old man, a cosmic policeman who snoops around to find evildoers and punishes them, a private possession to be carried to guarantee personal prosperity and happiness, and an absolute creator who withdrew to heaven to watch his universe.

Though we surely have no sympathy for such defective and even sacrilegious views of God, how much do we really know about God's character? And how then can we worship Him intelligently and meaningfully? It has been suggested that we too best worship God when we meditate on His attributes; that is, when we thank Him for His omniscience, omnipotence, and omnipresence; for His holiness, justice, love, goodness, faithfulness, mercy, and truth; and for His infinity, eternity, incomprehensibility, and immutability.

Confession (vv. 6-7). The more Nehemiah thought on God the more he became aware of the sin of the people that prevented God from acting on their behalf. Perhaps he remembered the words of the Psalmist, "If I regard iniquity in my heart, the Lord will not hear me" (Ps. 66:18). Nehemiah applied this to the nation, and openly confessed "the sins of the Children of Israel" (v. 6). Furthermore, he humbly identified himself with the people in the apportionment of the blame, as did Moses (Ex. 34:9), Ezra (Ezra 9:10), and Daniel (Dan. 9:5).

Nehemiah's confession moved from the general to the specific. He acknowledged that the sin was an offense against God: "We have dealt very corruptly against Thee" (1:7). We seem to hear an echo of David's confession of his dark sin against Bathsheba and Uriah. When he finally realized it was a sin against God, David cried, "Against Thee, Thee only, have I sinned, and done this evil in Thy sight" (Ps. 51:4).

Nehemiah specifically confessed that their sins were against the commandments, statutes, and judgments of the Law of Moses (v. 7). He demonstrated clear theological insight into the plight of his people. The basic problems were not their Persian captors nor the pitiable condition of the remnant in Jerusalem. He penetrated directly to the root of the matter—the Jews were suffering as a result of their sins.

And what are God's people today expected to do when they sin? The answer is clear—we are to judge ourselves (1 Cor. 11:31) and confess our sins to the Lord (1 John 1:9).

A Sunday School teacher gave her class a long talk on sin, prayer, and confession of sin. When she had finished the lesson, she asked little Kimberly, "What do we have to do before the Lord will forgive us?" "Sin!" replied Kimberly confidently.

Petition (vv. 8-11). Nehemiah then appealed to God, imploring Him to honor covenant promises made to Moses. "Remember . . . the word that Thou commandest Thy servant Moses . . . 'If ye transgress, I will scatter you . . . but if you turn unto Me . . . yet will I gather [thee]' " (vv. 8-9). He had in mind such passages as Leviticus 26:27-45, Deuteronomy 4:25-31, and 2 Chronicles 6:36-39 when he reminded God of what He had promised. Nehemiah knew that effective prayer is always based on the promises of God.

But hadn't God already fulfilled these promises? After all, the people had returned under Zerubbabel (536 B.C.) and under Ezra (444 B.C.). Nehemiah apparently felt that the promises had not been completely fulfilled, however, since the Jews in the land were still enduring hardship and reproach. His petition was for the people to be fully established under the blessing of God in the land.

Nehemiah not only reminded God of what He had said (vv. 8-9) but also of what He had done (v. 10). He reminded God that these afflicted people in Jerusalem were "Thy people, whom Thou has redeemed." The great redemption of Israel out of Egypt made them uniquely the people of God.

Can there be greater comfort and strength for the present, greater encouragement to pray for immediate needs, than to reflect on how a loving Father has dealt with us in the past? He has redeemed us and promised to bless us. What more do we need to encourage us to trust Him for today?

Gathering momentum, the prayer came to a climax as Nehemiah voiced a specific request, "Prosper, I pray Thee, Thy servant this day, and grant him mercy in the sight of this man" (v. 11). This great prayer began with thoughts of God, moved on to confession of sin, embraced the needs of the entire remnant in Jerusalem, then narrowed down to the definite request of an individual.

As Nehemiah prayed, it became apparent that he was to be the answer to his own prayer. As one writer stated, "The man who bathed the broken walls of Jerusalem with prayer would now employ his dedicated skills in rebuilding the ruins."

In order to carry out the plan that had been forming in Nehemiah's mind, he needed to gain release from his strategic position in the court as cupbearer to the king, a release which might be difficult, if not impossible, to secure apart from God's intervention. And for this he prayed.

Nehemiah was totally willing to place his own ambitions and abilities at God's disposal. He reminds us of Henry Martyn (1781-1812), who, following a brilliant student career at Cambridge, rejected several opportunities in order to go to the mission field. He prayed, "Here am I, Lord; send me to the ends of the earth, send me to the rough, the savage pagans of the wilderness; send me from all that is called comfort in earth; send me even to death itself if it be but in Thy service and in Thy kingdom." And so he labored for Christ in India and in Persia, only to become ill and die at the early age of 31.

As Nehemiah contemplated leaving a life of luxury in Persia for one of hardship in Palestine he might have prayed a prayer similar to one by Amy Carmichael (quoted from *Storms and Star Light* by V. Raymond Edman):

From prayer that asks that I may be
    Sheltered from winds that beat on Thee,
    From fearing when I should aspire,
    From faltering when I should climb higher,
    From silken self, O Captain, free
    Thy soldier who would follow Thee.

From subtle love of softening things,
    From easy choices, weakenings—
    Not thus are spirits fortified;
    Not this way went the Crucified.
    From all that dims Thy Calvary,
    O Lamb of God, deliver me.

Give me love that leads the way,
    The faith that nothing can dismay,
    The hope no disappointments tire,
    The passion that will burn like fire.
    Let me not sink to be a clod;
    Make me Thy fuel, Flame of God.

2
A Hero in the Making

It has been said that we are living in an age without heroes, and one observer declared, "It is questionable whether any society can avoid stagnation, if not disintegration, without them" (E. E. Jennings, *An Anatomy of Leadership* [New York: Harper & Brothers, 1960], p. 2).

Nehemiah is easily identifiable as the hero of his day. But how did it happen? Did he plan it that way? (From Richard C. Halverson's newsletter, "Perspective," October 26, 1977.)

The hero does not set out to be one.
He is probably more surprised than others by such recognition.
He was there when the crisis occurred . . .
And he responded as he always had in any situation.
He was simply doing what had to be done!
Faithful where he was in his duty there . . .
He was ready when the crisis arose.
Being where he was supposed to be . . .
Doing what he was supposed to do . . .
Responding as was his custom . . .
To circumstances as they developed . . .
Devoted to duty—he did the heroic!"

Chapter 2 shows how Nehemiah came to occupy the role of a

hero in ancient Israel. It is a chapter of transition, for Nehemiah moves from Persia to Palestine, from the position of servant to a heathen king, to be a recognized leader of his own people.

Petitioning the King (2:1-8)

Four long months, from Chisleu (1:1) to Nisan (2:1), Nehemiah prayed, rehearsing and repeating the prayer recorded in chapter 1. Hanani and the other Jewish travelers probably despaired of any results from their woeful description to Nehemiah of the condition of Jerusalem. No doubt they asked the question we too are curious about, "Why the delay?" Some have suggested that since Persian kings had several cupbearers who served in rotation, Nehemiah was not on duty for this period. Others feel the king was absent from Susa, spending the winter at another of his palaces, perhaps at Babylon. Nehemiah may have been waiting for a suitable occasion to approach the king, such as at the beginning of a new year when requests would be more readily granted. Or better yet, Nehemiah was no doubt waiting for God to answer and give him the right opportunity to speak to the king about his burden. Saints of God will testify that our timetable and God's often do not coincide. While we may want instant answers, God's timing is perfect—and His delays are not denials.

Nehemiah's opportunity came in a most unexpected, and even frightening way. Apparently, he had been able to master his grief for months while in the king's presence, but now the time came when his self-control had broken down and his face betrayed a heavy heart. The king was quick to notice, and, making an accurate diagnosis, concluded that Nehemiah's sufferings were not physical but in the heart or mind (v. 2).

The response of Nehemiah to the king's observation was twofold. First, he was "very sore afraid" (v. 2b). And for a good reason. Persian subjects were expected to be supremely happy when looking on the face of the king and risked severe punishment if they registered sadness in his presence. In addition, Nehemiah was about to request permission to leave the king and depart to another place. That too was unheard-of and dangerous! Furthermore, Nehemiah wanted permission to repair the destruction Artaxerxes had recently authorized (see 1:3 and Ezra 4:7-23). The cupbearer may well have reflected on the fact that while it was hard to get into a Persian court, it was harder still to get out!

Nehemiah responded to the king's penetrating question with a direct and truthful answer (v. 3). He explained that he could not be other than sad with the city of his ancestors lying desolate. But Artaxerxes sensed that there was more than this on Nehemiah's mind and he pursued the matter by inviting his servant to tell the whole story (v. 4).

The critical moment had arrived. This was the opening, the opportunity Nehemiah had prayed for. Knowing the intense importance of his reply to the future destiny of his people, and believing in the intervention of God in times of need, Nehemiah paused to pray (v. 4b). It was a short prayer, for we can be sure the king would not tolerate a long period of silence. But then, prayers need not be long to be effective (see Matt. 14:29-31). Perhaps this prayer was simply the petition at the end of the previous chapter, "Prosper, I pray Thee, Thy servant this day, and grant him mercy in the sight of this man" (1:11b).

One writer says, "The brief and sudden prayer reaches heaven as an arrow shot from the bow, but it goes right home, because he who lets it off in his surprise is a good workman, well practiced. This ready prayer only springs to the lips of a man who lives in a daily habit of praying" (W. F. Adeney, *Ezra, Nehemiah & Esther* [New York: Hodder & Stoughton, n.d], p. 191).

Nehemiah's swift, silent prayer brought quick results. Having prayed to God, he then talked to the king and made three requests. God may have put these carefully chosen words in Nehemiah's mouth at this time, but it is more likely that as Nehemiah prayed during the months after he first became aware of the needs in Judah, a plan formulated in his mind. He did his homework, carefully thinking through what he would need for such an expedition and how he could best express this to the king when the opportunity came.

Nehemiah first asked that the king send him to repair the ruins of Jerusalem (v. 5). This was a daring request because it was a gigantic task. What if he failed? But God had placed this burden on the heart of Nehemiah and he was confident that the One who had called him to this task would enable him to accomplish it. He always does.

Before granting the request, the king inquired how long the

cupbearer would be gone (v. 6). Nehemiah set a time for his return. While we later learn he was away for 12 years (5:14) it is possible he requested periodic extensions and may not have asked for such a lengthy leave at this time. Nehemiah did not request that he be made governor of Jerusalem, though subsequent narratives show that this was his position and the appointment may well have taken place on this occasion.

Nehemiah's second request was for letters of safe conduct (v. 7). These letters, addressed to the Persian governors west of the Euphrates River, would allow him to pass through their territories on the way to Jerusalem without being hindered.

The third request was for a letter addressed to Asaph, keeper of the king's forest, which was no doubt near Jerusalem. Nehemiah wished to secure timber from this preserve for the citadel or fortress that protected the area of the temple, for the construction of gates and towers along the walls, and for the building of his own official residence (v. 8).

It is said that Alexander the Great had a famous general to whom he had given permission to draw on the royal treasury for any amount. On one occasion, this general made a draft for such an enormous sum that the treasurer refused to honor the draft till he consulted the emperor. Going into his presence, the treasurer reported the general's action. "Did you honor the draft?" asked the emperor. "No, I refused till I had seen your majésty because the amount was so great." The emperor was indigant. "Do you not know," replied the emperor, "that he honors me and my kingdom by making a large draft?"

So Nehemiah honored Artaxerxes by making large requests— and all of them were granted. Some have suggested that there was good reason for the king to change his mind between the time he ordered the building activity in Jerusalem to cease (Ezra 4) and the time he gave Nehemiah permission to go for that same purpose. Secular sources indicate unrest in Egypt and on Cyprus, and Artaxerxes may well have desired a governor in Judah of Nehemiah's stature.

But Nehemiah does not attribute the granting of his requests to this political motivation, nor to his own wisdom or cleverness, but gives God the glory, "And the king granted me, according to the good hand of my God upon me" (v. 8b).

One sure sign of spiritual maturity is the ability and willingness to recognize the hand of God in the affairs of life. What a contrast to this is seen in the words of Gordon Liddy, a Watergate conspirator, when he was released from prison. Liddy declared, "I have found within myself all I need and all I ever shall need. I am a man of great faith, but my faith is in George Gordon Liddy. I have never failed me."

Arriving at the City (2: 9-11)

Ezra's expedition had journeyed from Babylon to Jerusalem in 458 B.C. Numbering about 1,800 persons, the caravan also transported valuable treasure and yet refused a military escort (see Ezra 8:22). Fourteen years later, Nehemiah made the trip but there were vast differences: a much smaller company, no valuables, and a military escort (v. 9). The presence of a military escort should not infer that Nehemiah's faith was weaker. The text indicates that the escort was a decision of the king, no doubt to protect and enhance the authority of his newly appointed governor. Traveling lighter, it is suggested that Nehemiah's company took the shorter route from Susa to Tadmore through Damascus. Following the Jordan Valley to Jericho they would avoid the Samaritan community and arrive in Jerusalem without encountering any opposition.

Nehemiah must have been welcomed by Ezra and others but the text is strangely silent concerning this and mentions only that the enemies of the Jews in Samaria heard of the arrival of the new governor (v. 10). "The knot of desperate men collected in the old Israelite capital, and animated with a bitter hatred of the Jewish community . . . saw with sullen disappointment the coming of a man who was likely to advance the welfare of their detested neighbors" (George Rawlinson, *Ezra and Nehemiah*, p. 94). Their deep concern stemmed in part from their fear that Jerusalem might regain her preeminence in Palestine, a position then enjoyed by the rival city of Samaria. Thus, united in their animosity for the Jews were Sanballat, an inhabitant of Beth-horan and apparently governor of Samaria, and Tobiah, probably a Jewish-Ammonite governor.

Nehemiah did not plunge immediately into his work. He stated, "So I came to Jerusalem, and was there three days" (v. 11). What

did he do for those three days? Probably, they were primarily
days of rest. Even by the shorter route the journey from Susa was
rigorous and required at least two months. Furthermore, from
what we already know about this man we can be sure he spent
considerable time in prayer and planning. He must have reflected
on the events of the past six months and thought of how a burden
had been transformed into a vision. But now that he was on the
scene was he facing an impossible dream? After all, no one else
had been able to restore Jerusalem in almost 150 years. Many
before him had said, "It can't be done." But with God's help
Nehemiah purposed to accomplish the impossible.

Inspecting the Ruins (2:12-16)

After three quiet days in Jerusalem, Nehemiah's first move was to
go out under cover of darkness to inspect the condition of the
city walls. No doubt it was in bright moonlight that the cautious
leader took his famous midnight ride. Since he probably arrived
in Jerusalem from the north he would already have observed the
state of the walls there and if he resided in the southwestern part
of the city he had ample time to view the western wall. His
concern was to inspect secretly the southern and eastern walls of
Jerusalem.

Leaving the city with a few servants, Nehemiah passed through
the Valley Gate opening into the Valley of Hinnom. The small
party then went counterclockwise along the south wall. Passing
the Dung Gate, through which the town's refuse was carried, it
was sorrowfully observed that the walls on this side of Jerusalem
were "broken down" and the gates were "consumed with fire" (v.
13). At the southeast corner of the city where the Valley of
Hinnom joins the Valley of the Kidron, and near the Gate of the
Fountain and a reservoir called the "kings pool," the heaps of
rubble and piles of stones obstructed passage. Nehemiah was
forced to dismount, and he continued on foot up the Kidron
Valley along the Brook Kidron in order to view the eastern walls.
He then seems to have retraced his steps, reentering the city by
means of his exit, the Gate of the Valley (v. 15).

But why, while others slept, did Nehemiah prowl along the
ruined walls? The reasons may have been many but it seems he
was not content with hearsay evidence such as he had received

in Persia. He had to see for himself. He needed the cooperation of many people to do the job of rebuilding and would not think of asking for their help till he had firsthand information of the size and nature of the task.

Nehemiah used his nighttime circuit of the walls to assemble the necessary information. If the report of the Jewish travelers moved him to tears (see 1:4), what must have been the effect of seeing the dismal desolation of Jerusalem with his own eyes? Alan Redpath, a noted Christian author and speaker, wrote,

Imagine his grief of heart as he stumbled among those ruins of what was once a great and mighty fortress! Whenever a real work of God is to be done . . . some faithful, burdened servant has to take a journey such as Nehemiah took, to weep in the night over the ruins, to wrestle in some dark Gethsemane in prayer . . . Are our hearts ever stirred like that? Have you ever lost one hour of sleep over the tragic spiritual dearth of your church and your city? Has it ever kept you awake? And have you cried, "O God, what can I do about this thing?" (*Victorious Christian Service* [Westwood, New Jersey: Fleming H. Revell Co., 1963], pp. 44-45.)

Rallying the People (2:17-20)

It was a former president of Columbia University who said, "There are three kinds of people in the world—those who don't know what's happening, those who watch what's happening, and those who make things happen."

Nehemiah clearly falls into the third category of individuals, as this passage shows. There was no more time for weeping and lamenting; it was now time to act. Assembling the nobles and others, Nehemiah laid before them the plans he had formulated on the basis of his night ride around the walls.

He identified himself with the people and called on them to recognize and acknowledge the unhappy condition in which they were living (v. 17a). The place to begin was with the problem. Unless their plight was freely admitted, no remedy could be adopted.

Nehemiah exhorted the people to act, reminding them that because of the run-down condition of the city they were held in contempt and scorn by their neighbors (v. 17b). For the people of God this was intolerable, and even constituted a reproach on God Himself.

Finally, Nehemiah encouraged his hearers by passing on to them two facts which lay at the very foundation of his confident faith. First, aware that God's hand had been on him, he assured the people that God was in this project. Further, he affirmed that he was acting on the authority of the king (v. 18a).

The response of the people was electric. Echoing Nehemiah's challenge they said, "Let us rise up and build" (v. 18). Thus was overcome that first great obstacle to any work for God—inertia. The very people who had been so lethargic and indifferent were now ready to get involved in the task, and all because of a God-sent, God-inspired leader. One writer has well said, "Effective Christian service demands a Spirit-filled leader whose vision and self-sacrifice inflame those who are sharing in the work of God."

But the enemy had been keeping a close and jealous watch on Jerusalem and were quick to challenge the newly adopted plan of action (v. 19). Sanballat and Tobiah were joined by Geshem the Arabian, perhaps the head of a group of Arab soldiers quartered at Samaria by Sanballat.

First, the enemy openly mocked the Jews, ridiculing their efforts to rebuild the walls. Adventuresome and courageous pioneers have often faced the laughter of jealous observers. "The first American steamboat took 32 hours to go from New York to Albany. People laughed. The horse and buggy passed the early motorcar as if it were standing still. (It usually was.) People laughed. The first electric light bulb was so dim people had to use a gas lamp to see it. They laughed. The first airplane came down 59 seconds after it left the ground. People laughed" (*Bible Knowledge*, Wheaton: Scripture Press, 1968, p. 63).

The enemy also charged that Nehemiah and his followers were rebuilding the walls as a part of a plot to rebel against the king of Persia.

Nehemiah's answer was brief but firm (v. 20). He ignored the charge that they were rebelling against the king and resolutely declared that they were staking everything on God—"The God of heaven, He will prosper us." Further, Nehemiah served notice that from that time forward neither the enemy nor their descendants would be able to prey on the Jews, for they would no longer be able to expect tribute or exercise authority over the people of God in Jerusalem.

Looking back over this chapter, principles of effective leadership come to the surface in almost every verse. Some of these principles as exemplified in Nehemiah's character and conduct are:

He established a reasonable and attainable goal
He had a sense of mission
He was willing to get involved
He rearranged his priorities in order to accomplish his goal
He patiently waited for God's timing
He showed respect to his superior
He prayed at crucial times
He made his request with tact and graciousness
He was well prepared and thought of his needs in advance
He went through proper channels
He took time (three days) to rest, pray, and plan
He investigated the situation firsthand
He informed others only after he knew the size of the problem
He identified himself as one with the people
He set before them a reasonable and attainable goal
He assured them God was in the project
He displayed self-confidence in facing obstacles
He displayed God's confidence in facing obstacles
He did not argue with opponents
He was not discouraged by opposition
He courageously used the authority of his position.

With such a leader at the helm of affairs in Jerusalem, small wonder the impossible dream soon became a reality. Our prayer today should be that God will raise up more like Nehemiah to serve as Christian leaders. Karl Jaspers has said, "The power of leadership appears to be declining everywhere" (quoted from *The Making of a Christian Leader* by Ted Engstrom, Grand Rapids: Zondervan Publishing House, 1976, p. 12). The spiritual needs of our world cry out for more Nehemiahs.

3
Mission Impossible:
How to Accomplish It

During the defense of the Philippine Bataan Peninsula in World War II, one of the commanding officers lined up a company of his men and asked for a volunteer to go on a dangerous mission. Anyone willing to serve in this capacity was to step forward two paces. Glancing at his memorandum for a moment, he looked up, and exclaimed in dismay, "What, not a single man?" Quickly his aide explained, "You do not understand, sir. The entire line stepped forward two paces!"

Nehemiah experienced a similar response to his challenge to the people of Jerusalem to join him in a mission impossible—they stepped forward from every sector, every walk of life, to follow his leadership. President Eisenhower said, "Leadership is the ability to get a person to do what you want him to do, when you want it done, in a way you want it done, because he wants to do it." The *Harvard Business Review* described an effective executive as one who could build cooperative effort within the team he leads (Sept.-Oct. 1974, p. 91).

It was in large measure the effective leadership of Nehemiah that accounted for the incredible accomplishments in Jerusalem. History scarcely knows anything like it. Ancient Rome and Carthage, it is true, were rebuilt after being destroyed by fire and invaders. Modern cities, too, have known spectacular restorations after being leveled by aerial bombardment; yet in all such cases the human and monetary resources were abundant. In ancient

Jerusalem the feat was accomplished by those who were few in number, limited in resources, and surrounded by enemies who tried to block their efforts.

Nehemiah chapter 3 has been treated in a variety of ways. Because it gives us the most detailed specifications of the wall of Jerusalem to be found in the Bible, some writers in their treatment of the chapter dwell only on the topography of the ancient city. Others, apparently feeling that the blessing justifies the means, all but ignore the historical information and allegorize the gates of the city so that spiritual lessons may be taught. Still others concentrate on the 38 names mentioned in the chapter or only emphasize leadership principles. Perhaps a combination of several of these approaches will give us the best understanding of the chapter.

The Psalmist wrote, "The Lord loveth the gates of Zion more than all the dwellings of Jacob. Glorious things are spoken of thee, O city of God" (Ps. 87:2-3). Says Professor Adeney:

> No city was ever more favored by Heaven, and no city was ever more afflicted. Hers were the most magnificent endowments, the highest ideals, the fairest promises; hers too was the most miserable failure. Her beauty ravaged, her sanctity defiled, her light extinguished, her joy turned into bitterness, Heaven's bride has been treated as the scum of the streets. And now, after being abused by her own children, shattered by the Babylonian, outraged by the Syrian, demolished by the Romans, the city which stoned her prophets and clamoured successfully for the death of her Saviour has again revived. . . . The witchery of this wonderful city fascinates us today, and the very syllables of her name "Jerusalem" sound strangely sweet and ineffably sad—"most musical, most melancholy" (W. F. Adeney, *Ezra, Nehemiah & Esther*, pp. 233-34).

Nehemiah was determined that this city, so highly favored and so long afflicted, be restored in beauty and security. David sang, "Jerusalem is builded as a city that is compact together" (Ps. 122:3), but now it was lying in desolation, its ruined walls and collapsed fortifications exposing her people to being ravaged and scattered by the enemy.

Though the succinct account of the building activity in chapter 3 does not mention the prior organizational work of Nehemiah, there can be no doubt that he spent long hours getting all in readiness for the actual work to begin.

It is recognized that a universal trait of leadership is the ability to "cut the problems down to size." And Nehemiah did precisely that. He divided the wall into sections and assigned individuals and groups to the different portions. Each one had a specific task and knew that what he was doing was part of an overall plan. No one person could do the whole job, not even Nehemiah; but when everyone worked together, the most difficult task could be successfully completed. This is the pattern for today as well: there must be team effort in the local church, on the mission field, and in the Christian school.

The chapter, in tracing the work, takes us on a counterclockwise tour around the city wall. While it is difficult to locate every specified gate, tower, or stretch of wall, the general route is clear. And further archeological light may soon be available. Says archeologist Hershel Shanks, "What the stock market is to Wall Street and government to Washington, archeology is to Jerusalem. It is full of archeological talk and archeological gossip, of new finds and ideas and speculations" (*The Biblical Archaeological Review*, Vol. III, No. 4, December, 1977, p. 1).

The North Wall (3:1-5)

The Sheep Gate (vv. 1-2). The work of repair and rebuilding began near the northeast corner of the wall at the Sheep Gate. Since it is located not far from the temple and sheep market, it is commonly believed that animals for sacrifice passed through this gate.

This was an area in which the priests had a special interest, and we are encouraged as we observe that the first to respond to Nehemiah's appeal to build was Eliashib, the high priest, who led the other priests by setting his hand to the task. But was it not beneath the dignity of the exalted spiritual leader of the nation to clear away rubble, to carry heavy stones and set them in place in the wall? Apparently, this did not cross the minds of the priests and high priests who set such a striking example for all of the people.

Another unusual feature of this facet of the work was that the priests sanctified their task. That is, they dedicated the repaired gate, wall, and defense towers to God. While the formal dedication ceremony was not be be held for some time, the priests wanted to declare at this time their solemn belief that the very stone and timber of Jerusalem belonged to God, and that unless God blessed the city with His presence, even secure walls and gates would not keep the people safe.

The Fish Gate (vv. 3-5). The description of the building operation moves westward and we are told of the work at the Fish Gate and adjoining walls. Located in the north near the modern Damascus Gate, it was probably so named because merchants from Tyre regularly brought in their fish to sell in the nearby market.

The phrase "next to them" recurs in this section and throughout the chapter as another indication that the entire operation was carefully organized by Nehemiah. Even though it was a volunteer program, it was far from haphazard in its operation. The leader was confident of what he was doing, and every individual who participated knew precisely where he belonged and what was expected of him.

It is a delight to read of the sons of Hassenaah, Meremoth, Meshullam, Zadok, and the Tekoites, and envision them working happily and heartily at their assigned posts. But then the harmony of the scene is marred by the painful exception of the nobles of Tekoa, "But their nobles put not their necks to the work of their Lord" (v. 5b). The citizens of Tekoa, a village 10 miles south of Jerusalem, took a double share in the rebuilding efforts (see vv. 5, 27). Why did the nobles hold back? Did they think this kind of work was beneath their dignity? Did they distrust the leaders in Jerusalem?

Interestingly, Nehemiah apparently did not allow their sullen opposition to become an issue. He worked with those who shared his vision and were willing to cooperate.

Out of one of the wars of history comes the story of a captain who in the midst of a battle missed one of his men. He remembered that he had not seen him since they passed through a village a few miles away. When he was free to leave his men, he hurried back and after a quick search found the soldier walking about in a beautiful garden. He was court-martialed and his only defense was, "But I wasn't doing anything!" That, of course, was the very grounds of his conviction—in a time of conflict he was totally indifferent to the commands of his superior.

Soldiers and deserters; workers and shirkers. Both groups are with us today. Are we like the nobles of Tekoa who wanted the benefits of a rebuilt Jerusalem but refused to take an active part themselves in the work of the Lord?

The West Wall (3: 6-12)

The Old Gate (vv. 6-12). Located on the northwest wall, the Old Gate was probably the entrance to the old city. It is often identified with the Corner Gate (see 2 Kings 14:13 and 2 Chron. 26:9) and it stood between the Fish Gate and the Ephraim Gate (see Neh. 12:39).

An interesting assortment of people worked at this gate and the stretch of western wall beyond it. There were goldsmiths and perfumers (v. 8), men who normally did light, delicate work but who shared the burden of rebuilding Jerusalem's fortifications. And who can doubt that blistered hands and aching muscles were their lot as a result?

While the nobles of Tekoa stood aloof (v. 5), the nobles of Jerusalem got involved, leaving for a time their important administrative duties to set an example of cooperation and to have a part in this vital operation (vv. 9, 12).

Young women also left the comfort and security of their homes to work on the wall (v. 12), and they were given credit for doing so along with the men. Of course, if their fathers had no sons, their desire to help could be more easily understood since they would inherit his name and property (see Num. 36:8). Who knows what influence these couragaeous young women had in encouraging many other women to toil alongside the men? Ralph Turnbull comments,

> Florence Nightingale of England was a young woman of fashion and society. She heard the call of God and gave herself to the relief of the wounded and dying. Then, it was thought degrading and lowering for a gentle woman to engage in nursing. She changed all

that by her noble example and devotion. Out of her
service came the elevation of the nursing vocation . . .
and the inspiration of young women to give themselves
to the service of God. Paul, like Nehemiah, was mindful of those women who labored with him in the Gospel (Phil. 4:30). The women's work in the church and
for the kingdom of God is a noble one indeed (*The
Book of Nehemiah* [Grand Rapids: Baker Book House,
1968], p. 30).

We are told that this potpourri of people fortified Jerusalem
as far as "the broad wall" (v. 8) which was apparently doubly
reinforced at this point for greater protection. In 1970, Professor
Nachman Avigad of the Hebrew University in Jerusalem unearthed an impressive segment of this portion of the ancient city
wall dating to the time of Hezekiah (700 B.C.) and found that it
was 22 feet thick (*The Biblical Archaeology Review*, Vol. II, No.
1, March, 1976, p. 7).

The South Wall (3:13-14)

The Valley Gate (v. 13). Located at the southwest corner and
opening into the Valley of Hinnom, this gate was repaired by the
inhabitants of Zanoah, a village 13 miles west of Jerusalem. These
people also repaired the wall for a distance of some 1,500 feet
from the Valley Gate to the Dung Gate, a stretch that apparently
suffered much less damage than other parts and therefore could
be more easily and quickly repaired.

The Dung Gate (v. 14). The refuse of the town was carried out
the gate and burned in the Hinnom Valley. Would anyone volunteer to work at so lowly a site? A ruler from Beth-haccerem, a
village about three miles south of Jerusalem, took the job and
finished it. It does not appear that he was assisted by any great
number of helpers. Did they seek a more prestigious location in
which to invest their efforts?

The East Wall (3:15-31)

The Fountain Gate (vv. 15-25). When Nehemiah arrived in Jerusalem and made his nighttime survey, he found the area of the
Fountain Gate in almost complete ruin (see 2:14). The gate and

section of the eastern wall following it were now repaired up to the Water Gate.

In addition to the gate and walls, mention is also made of a number of other significant features of this area. Since the time of Hezekiah, Jerusalem's water supply had been safeguarded even in time of siege by a tunnel dug by the king's workmen out of solid rock. Two crews of workmen, one starting at the Spring of Gihon outside the walls, and the other starting at what is now the Pool of Siloam, performed this amazing feat and the water flowed from the spring to the pool (see 2 Kings 20:20). This Pool of Siloam, the wall that protected the reservior, and the stairs that descended from the upper city to the water supply are all described (v. 15). Likewise, the "sepulchres of David," believed to be the tombs of the kings of Judah, are mentioned in verse 16. Observers may now see the fascinating remains of these sites, and a major archeological dig sponsored by Jerusalem's Hebrew University is expected to turn the entire area into an archeological park.

Along the eastern section of the wall many workers toiled. Nehemiah knew them all and listed many by name. He especially commended Baruch who "earnestly" or "zealously" repaired the section of wall assigned to him. With a name meaning "blessed" Baruch was noted for his burning zeal and enthusiasm, a vivid contrast to the Tekoite nobles, and a man to be emulated in the service of God.

It is recorded that Benjamin and Hashub repaired "over against their house" (v. 23), an expression also found in verses 10 and 29. Cyril J. Barber comments:

In assessing the importance of this we find that Nehemiah took advantage of convenience. He did not have people "commuting" from one end of Jerusalem to another. This would have wasted time and reduced efficiency. It would also have made it difficult for the workers to be fed. Furthermore, in the event of an attack by their enemies, each man's concern would have been for his family. If his family were somewhere else in Jerusalem, he would have no way of protecting them. By arranging for each man to work close to his own home, Nehemiah made it easy for them to get to work, to be sustained while on the job, and to safeguard those who

were nearest and dearest to them. This relieved each worker
of any unnecessary anxiety. It also insured that each person
would put his best effort into what he was doing (Cyril J.
Barber, *Nehemiah and the Dynamics of Effective Leadership*, [Neptune, New Jersey: Loizeaux Brothers, 1976], p.
49).

The Water Gate (vv. 26-27). This gate was named for its prox-
imity to the Spring of Gihon. The Nethinims (temple servants)
and Tekoites labored in this section called the Ophel. Originally,
Ophel referred to the small hill or projection immediately south
of the Temple Mount, but later the name was used for the entire
eastern ridge. It was the site of the ancient Jebusite city captured
by David, a segment of whose ancient walls have been unearthed
recently. Ophel is outside the walls of modern-day Jerusalem.

It is the opinion of many archeologists that Nehemiah did not
follow the line of the old city wall on this eastern side of the
city, but that he abandoned the destroyed lower slope and built
his wall higher up on the fairly level crest of the hill. There the
modern-day observer can examine a portion of the wall rebuilt
by the temple servants and Tekoites.

The Horse Gate (v. 28). A third group of priests (see vv. 1,
22, 28) worked in the region of the Horse Gate that seems to
have been the entrance to the city for the palace traffic. It is
probably to be identified with the horses' entrance to the king's
house (2 Kings 11:16).

The East Gate (vv. 29-30). Continuing the northward direction
we come next to the East Gate, the entrance into the temple area
from the Mount of Olives and probably the ancient predecessor of
the modern Golden Gate.

The Miphkad Gate (v. 31). Sometimes referred to as the Muster
Gate and located at the northeast corner of the city, the Miphkad
Gate may have been the place for the mustering of troops and
guards. We gather from Nehemiah 12:39 that the Prison Gate was
also in this neighborhood.

The circuit of the wall was completed with reference to the
portion leading back to the Fish Gate, a segment restored by goldsmiths and merchants whose business was in the area near the
temple (v. 32).

Nehemiah is not mentioned in chapter 3. The focus is not on the leader but on the people. And yet who would dare suggest that Nehemiah was not on hand every day of this vital building program, making a daily trip around the walls, pausing at one place to encourage and stopping at another to lend a hand? The next three chapters give clear evidence of his vital involvement. But the spotlight is focused on the laborers themselves and the chapter gives a wonderful example of the Lord's people successfully working together.

Important principles for Christian service can be gleaned from this chapter:

1. The work of God should be carried on in an orderly and organized fashion. Paul wrote to the Corinthians, "Let all things be done decently and in order" (1 Cor. 14:40). Few better illustrations of that exhortation in action can be found in Scripture than in Nehemiah 3.

2. There must be a division of labor in the Lord's work. The leader or leaders simply cannot do it all, nor has that ever been God's purpose. In the church, for instance, it is clear that God gave gifted men so that the saints might be equipped for *their* work of ministering (Eph. 4:12).

3. The Lord's work requires the involvement of all kinds of people from different walks of life. Since we are told that every believer has some spiritual gift or gifts and that these are given for the common good (1 Cor. 12:7), sitting in the stands or remaining on the sidelines are not valid options. Rather, we are challenged to be active participants in His service (1 Cor. 15:58).

4. The Lord remembers and honors those who serve Him. Nehemiah 3 is filled with the names of the honored faithful and even includes some who were unfaithful. Perhaps it is a sample of what will be revealed at the Judgment Seat of Christ when the believers' records of service will be examined and some will be rewarded while others suffer loss (see 1 Cor. 3:13-15).

In the book *Daktar/Diplomat in Bangladesh*, Dr. Viggo Olsen tells of his work as a medical missionary in Bangladesh. On one occasion, he had assumed responsibility for building 4,000 houses for homeless people in that land. He wrote:

Having finished the Book of Ezra in my morning Bible

reading, I began the Book of Nehemiah. I spent every spare moment thinking through how to organize the brigade's work in such a way that we could actually complete the four thousand houses. . . . Early on the morning of April 15, as I read the tedious third chapter of Nehemiah, two principles suddenly leaped out of those pages at me—principles which showed me how the Bangladesh Brigade should be organized . . . I was struck that no expert builders were listed in the "Holy Land Brigade"; there were priests, priests' helpers, goldsmiths, perfume-makers, and women, but no expert builders or carpenters were named. If those amateurs could complete the wall of Jerusalem in fifty-two days, we also, despite our lack of expertise should be able to complete our work in fifty-two days, almost exactly the time we had left to work . . . Nehemiah 3 had strengthened my impression that instead of concentrating our men to work together in one or two villages, we must send out multiple teams to work simultaneously in many villages.

The Nehemiah passages also imparted another principle; instead of each team doing the same small phase of work, assemby-line style, in village after village, each team must, instead, manage and supervise the total operation in its target villages from initial survey to final inspection and completed houses. With these principles as our guidelines, we put together our house building system (V. B. Olsen, *Daktar/Diplomat in Bangladesh* [Chicago: Moody Press, 1973], pp. 373ff.).

In seven weeks they finished the 4,000 houses—and the plan of organization came from Nehemiah 3. Far from containing merely a tiresome recitation of facts about a building program, this chapter gives a valuable plan of action for people anywhere and at any time.

4
What to do
When Under Attack

"Great changes in the history of an organization or society generally result from the innovative efforts of a few superior individuals," wrote Eugene E. Jennings (*An Anatomy of Leadership* [New York: Harper & Brothers, 1960], p. 1). And great changes were taking place in Jerusalem largely due to the consecrated abilities and dynamic leadership of Nehemiah. In fact, his heart probably throbbed with excitement as he made the daily circuit and saw the progress on the project. Chapter 4, however, informs us that the work was accomplished only in the face of severe opposition. The opposition continued till the walls were finished—and even after.

How do we account for such vicious and unrelenting attacks as are recorded in the next three chapters of this book, attacks that originated both externally and internally?

Simply, that Satan tries to oppose the work of God in any way he can. In this case, he launched an all-out effort to stop the Jerusalem building program. Nehemiah might have undertaken to rebuild walls anywhere else in the Persian Empire and he would have escaped the opposition of the enemy. But Jerusalem was the center of God's earthly purposes and to build its walls was an unpardonable offense. Satan has always tried to oppose what God purposes to do through His earthly people, Israel.

Paul warned believers of the "wiles of the devil" (Eph. 6:11) and stated, "We are not ignorant of his devices" (2 Cor. 2:11).

Sometimes, Satan operates in the open (1 Peter 5:8) and other times he camouflages himself (2 Cor. 11:14). In any case, we would do well never to minimize his power and program. Harold J. Okenga in his book, *Faithful in Christ Jesus*, said, "Any misunderstanding, any underrating, or underestimating of the enemy we fight is fatal. He is powerful, worldwide, tenacious, ruthless, brutal, persistent, and seeks but one end, the destruction of your soul."

Close attention to Nehemiah's experiences will teach us more about the evil devices of the enemy and our resources for overcoming them.

Opposition by Mockery (4:1-6)

The problem (vv.1-4). Nehemiah had seemed impervious to the blustering gibes of his opponents shortly after his arrival in Jerusalem (see 2:19-20), but now they become more intense. Sanballat was furious when he observed the progress on the wall, because a secure and independent Jerusalem would undermine his authority and might even mean economic loss for Samaria if trade were attracted to the restored city.

Gathering his small army outside Jerusalem, Sanballat loudly asked a series of sarcastic questions (v. 2) and the army no doubt laughed in derision. Do these feeble Jews actually believe they can build this wall with their inadequate materials and a God who can't help them anyway?

Tobiah then stepped forward to take up the jest, declaring insultingly that if one of the foxes that prowled the nearby hills should jump on the wall it would collapse (v. 3)—and again the army laughed with malicious glee.

Ridicule is not an innocent weapon, but is subtle, effective, and always modern. Alan Redpath wrote:

When the Christian dares to say that the only hope of the world is in the Gospel of God's redeeming grace, the whole force of modern civilization and education lines up against him and says, "You, with your feeble prayer meetings. You, with your silly little plan of getting people converted one by one. How can that possibly stand alongside our great socializing economic program in which a whole world can be

revolutionized in a few years? You feeble little lot!" The
world judges everything by size, by headlines, by imposing
schemes, by vast advertisements, and it pours contempt upon
the feeble little flock of the people of God. "You have no
intellect. You are out of date. You have no money. You
have no status" (Alan Redpath, *Victorious Christian Service,*
[Westwood, New Jersey: Fleming H. Revell Co., 1963], pp.
71-72).

A stark example of vicious ridicule of the Lord's work can be
seen in the following reprint from the *Pontiac Observer* of several
years ago commenting on the work of Inter-Varsity Christian
Fellowship:

A group of (doubtlessly) well-meaning fanatics have become
established at the fast-expanding Oakland University in
Rochester, Michigan. Already sizeable in number and tagged
"The Inter-Varsity," its members differ from other students,
and call themselves Christians (a term used to describe followers of a country preacher who died centuries ago). They
even claim that this teacher is at present living in the area.
Membership is open to all who hold this teacher to be their
"savior!" One wonders how a society can thrive on such an
insecure basis. Meetings are held most any time and place
(even in dormitory rooms and apartments, they say) on
subjects such as: *Faith—Is It the Surrender of Intellect?* or
Encounter with Christ. The spread of this sedition can only
be halted by challenging them at all opportunities, in their
group meetings or in the university, and proving to them how
unfounded is the idea of theirs that this Christ is not in fact
dead but is alive among us (from *Inter-Varsity News,* January, 1967).

The response (vv. 4-6). In the midst of the raucous laughter
a quiet voice was heard, the voice of Nehemiah, who chose not to
engage in argument or debate with his enemies but to lay the
whole matter out before the Lord. Praying over problems is, after
all, the best solution.
But the prayer of Nehemiah has been a puzzle to many. It ap-

pears harsh and vindictive. One writer stated, "We shudder as we read his terrible words . . . for the moment he lost his self-possession." Can we really believe this prayer was expressed in a fit of temper? There must be a better explanation for the fact that Nehemiah prayed for the reproach of the enemies to be turned back on them even to the extent of their experiencing the bitterness of exile (v. 4). He even went so far as to ask that God not forgive their sins (v. 5).

This prayer, similar to the imprecatory psalm that appealed to God to pour out His wrath, was uttered during the economy of the Mosaic law which allowed men to seek vengeance for injury on the basis of "eye for eye, tooth for tooth, hand for hand, foot for foot, burning for burning, wound for wound, stripe for stripe" (Ex. 21:24-25). Of course, the prayer is hardly a model for today when we are exhorted to "overcome evil with good," permitting God to bring vengeance as He sees fit (see Rom. 12:19-21). However, if the pronoun is properly supplied in the expression, "for they have provoked *Thee* to anger before the builders" (v. 5b), then it is clear that Nehemiah saw the Jews' enemies as God's enemies and His honor as being involved in this attack on His people. Their malicious mockery was blashphemy, and Nehemiah prayed that God would vindicate Himself by judging them.

Nehemiah's response to his enemies was not only prayer but also persistence in the work (v. 6). Calvin Coolidge said, "Press on. Nothing can take the place of persistence. Talent will not. Nothing is more common than unsuccessful men with talent. Genius will not. Unrewarded genius is almost a proverb. Education will not. The world is full of educated derelicts. Persistence and determination alone are overwhelmingly powerful."

Surrounded by ridicule, Nehemiah led his people steadfastly forward in their work till they had the wall halfway up (v. 6). It can be surmised that Nehemiah was keenly aware of the seriousness of the opposition and that it was a part of his strategy to get the walls rebuilt as quickly as possible. The task was soon half completed because "the people had a mind to work" (v. 6). The persistence and dedication of Nehemiah infected the workers and it appears that even the enemies were startled, as well as chagrined, by their rapid progress. Clearly, more drastic kinds of opposition would have to be set in motion.

Opposition by Conspiracy (4:7-9)

The problem (vv. 7-8). Jerusalem was surrounded: From the north (Samaria), south (Arabia), east (Ammon), and west (Ashdod, a city of Philistia) hostile forces came, stirred up by Sanballat and Tobiah. Angered because their earlier devices had failed, and finding that more than ridicule (v. 2) and foxes (v. 3) were needed to stop the work, the enemies of the Jews purposed to fight against Jerusalem and cause confusion within it. Since King Artaxerxes had authorized the rebuilding of the walls, open attack was out of the question. Apparently, the plan was to infiltrate and cause confusion by terrorist activity.

The response (v. 9). Would such a great show of strength frighten the Jews into inactivity? Would Nehemiah be intimidated?

A Marine sergeant said to his men, "We're surrounded by the enemy. Don't let one of them escape!"

So did Nehemiah's courage remain firm. Fully aware of his circumstances, he was also fully aware of his divine resources and he resorted to prayer. He did this at every important juncture of his life. Prior to this time, however, only his private prayers had been mentioned, whereas verse 9 records, "*We* made *our* prayer unto *our* God." Apparently, the prayerful spirit of the leader was infectious and his fellow citizens joined in beseeching Jehovah for strength and guidance. God was their present help in trouble (Ps. 46:1).

But prayer was not their only resource; they also set a continual watch day and night against the enemy (v. 9b). This was holding things in proper balance. To have prayed only would have been presumption and to have watched only would have indicated a lack of faith.

On one of D. L. Moody's trips across the Atlantic, a fire broke out in the hold of the ship. Moody and a friend joined the crew and other volunteers passing buckets of water to be thrown on the fire. The friend said to Moody, "Mr. Moody, let us go to the other end of the ship and pray." The common-sense evangelist replied, "No sir; we stand right here and pass buckets and pray hard all the time!"

Opposition by Defeatism (4:10-23)

The problem (vv. 10-12). A surprising development in the Jewish camp heightens the tension in the narrative—a spirit of discouragement and even defeatism gripped the workers. Men of Judah reported to Nehemiah that the laborers were suffering from exhaustion (v. 10). Furthermore, the piles of rubbish still loomed large and foreboding, particularly since the working force had been reduced to set up guards on the walls.

Nor only was the job too big, but so were the enemies. Sanballat started a whispering campaign among the Jews who lived in outlying areas. He said his forces would soon secretly attack those in Jerusalem, killing the workers and causing the progress on the walls to come to an end (vv. 11-12).

How would Nehemiah respond to discouragement among the workers—a subtle form of opposition?

There is a familiar legend that the devil puts his tools up for sale, marking each for public inspection with its appropriate sale price. Included were hatred, envy, jealousy, deceit, lying, and pride. Laid apart from these was a rather harmless looking but well-worn tool marked at an extremely high price.

A buyer pointed to this isolated implement and asked, "What is the name of this tool?"

"That is discouragement," the devil replied tersely.

"And why have you priced it so high?"

"Because it is more useful to me than the others. I can pry open a man's heart with that when I cannot get near to him with the other tools. Once inside, I can make him do whatever I choose. It is badly worn because I use it on almost everyone, since few people know it belongs to me."

The devil's price for discouragement was so high, it is said, that this tool was never sold. He continues to use it on God's people, causing spiritual growth to be stifled and many a worthwhile Christian project to grind to a halt.

The response (vv. 13-23). Nehemiah would not buckle under the enemies' assaults. He responded vigorously to the crisis and put the work on a war footing. A remarkable system of civil defense was set in motion. It involved seven measures:

1. The workers were armed and placed strategically on the wall (v. 13). This was essential because there was no professional Jewish army. In addition, men were posted according to their families because they would be spurred on to fight if they were defending their own homes.

2. The people were encouraged to trust God for protection (v. 14). One writer has said, "This was a fight for national survival." Nehemiah did not want them to trust in weapons but in the living God. He gave them a battle cry, "Remember the Lord!"

At various stages in our own national history soldiers have been rallied with such cries as "Remember the Alamo!"; "Remember the Maine!"; "Remember Pearl Harbor!" But the beleaguered Jews of Nehemiah's day had a more stirring cry to remind them of the One who could be counted on to meet their needs. And that was a great antidote to discouragement.

Someone once asked Charles Haddon Spurgeon if he ever got discouraged. He said, "Not for the last 20 years, I guess." When asked how he explained this, he said, "Because not 15 minutes ever go by without my thinking of Christ." It was the writer to a group of persecuted and discouraged Hebrew Christians who said, "For consider Him that endured such contradiction of sinners against Himself, lest ye be wearied and faint in your minds" (Heb. 12:3).

3. Nehemiah assigned his personal servants to help (v. 16). Half of them worked on the wall and the other half were heavily armed and ready to meet the first impact of the enemy.

4. Builders and burden-bearers carried weapons (vv. 17-18a). Since the builders needed both hands for their work they kept their swords on their sides. Those who carried baskets of debris on their heads held their weapons in one hand and with the other supported their loads.

5. An alarm system was instituted (vv. 18b-20). Since workmen and their helpers were scattered over a wide area, many beyond the reach of a human voice, a trumpeter with a ram's horn, or shofar, stood by the side of Nehemiah wherever he went. If Nehemiah became aware of an emergency and gave the order, the trumpet would be sounded and all would gather quickly at the danger spot, counting on God to fight for them.

6. Nighttime security was strengthened (v. 22). Not only did the builders work beyond sunset till the stars appeared (v. 21), but out-of-town workers were asked to remain in the city rather than returning to their homes, in order to help defend the walls in case of an attack.

7. Nehemiah exercised constant vigilance (v. 23). Josephus

commented on this verse by saying, "He himself [Nehemiah] made the rounds of the city by night, never tiring either through work or lack of food and sleep, neither of which he took for pleasure but as a necessity." Nehemiah was joined by his close associates in this watchfulness.

During the Reformation in Scotland, one of John Knox's co-workers paid tribute to him, "He can put more spirit into us than five hundred trumpets blowing at once." Nehemiah was that kind of leader. This chapter underscores again that he was a man of prayer (see vv. 4, 9), a man of faith (see vv. 4, 20), and a man of practical wisdom and common sense. While assuring the people that God would fight for them, he nonetheless led them in setting up an effective program of defense for Jerusalem.

Piety and practicality are not mutually exclusive qualities of life. They can be jointly practiced and Nehemiah has shown us how.

The late John E. Mitchell, Jr., for many years president of a manufacturing company in Dallas, Texas, was a modern-day Nehemiah. A widely recognized civic leader, Mr. Mitchell led a successful business. He was convinced that piety and practicality, religion and business, do mix. To illustrate this conviction, he told the following story:

Many years ago, in a little manufacturing company now much larger and fairly successful, there were two employees —one, a shipping clerk named Matlock and the other a night janitor named Washam. One of Washam's duties was to clean out the big brass cuspidors in the various offices. This was an onerous job, because in those days there was much tobacco chewing; and due to carelessness, poor marksmanship, and the nature of the commodity, the spittoons were usually filthy. One of the spittoons belonged to Matlock, a crotchety chap who took pride in his own work and was ready and quick to criticize what he regarded as poor work by another. Matlock became dissatisfied with the job Washam was doing on his cuspidor and told him so in a note which he attached one evening to the offending object. This note led to various exchanges, and a bitter feeling between the two men soon developed. The disagreement finally reached the point where neither would speak to the other when they chanced to meet in the evening.

The president of the company heard about the matter and decided to deal first with Washam. Accordingly, he remained at the plant one night to talk to the janitor on the job.

"Brother Washam," said the president, "I am greatly disappointed in you. You and I belong to the same church. We both profess to be Christians. Surely Christ would not be pleased with this silly quarrel over a cuspidor. Now, here is what I want you to do," he went on; "I want you to make Matlock's cuspidor the Number One item on your program every night. I want you to clean it and polish it as no cuspidor has ever been cleaned and polished before. I am going to stay here tonight long enough to help you with it myself. Let's remember that we are doing this job not for Matlock, but for the Lord. I believe the Lord has a special interest in this particular cuspidor. Let's do a really good job for Him."

Thus encouraged, the janitor went to work immediately on Matlock's brass cuspidor, and in half an hour it was a shining thing of beauty. In fact, Matlock could see the reflection of his face in its surface when he looked at it early the next morning. Matlock was greatly surprised. But especially was he surprised when he learned what had happened the night before; also he was embarrassed and ashamed. When the president brought the two men together in his office, they confessed that they had been acting like spoiled children. They shook hands then and there and began a friendship that endured for the rest of their lives.

Washam, Matlock, and the president of the company have been gone from the scene now these many years, but the symbol of the shining brass cuspidor lives on in the company they worked for. If you should visit the company today, you would notice on the walls of the different departments in all the factory buildings, and on all the desks in all the company's offices, a framed motto with these words printed in gold letters:

"And whatsoever ye do, do it heartily, as to the Lord, and not unto men" (Col. 3:23).

I recommend that motto as a basis for every Christian's business life, and for every company that professes to be Christian in its policies and activities. (John E. Mitchell, Jr., *The Christian in Business*. [Westwood, New Jersey: Fleming H. Revell Co., 1962], pp. 14-16).

5
Coping with the Fifth Column

Walt Kelly's cartoon figure "Pogo" said, "We have met the enemy and he is us!"

Nehemiah experienced the truth of this statement when he faced opposition from some on the inside. There is no mention of the enemies of the Jews with whom we have become familiar—Sanballat, Tobiah, and Geshem. They could rest, for their goal of stopping the rebuilding of the walls was about to be accomplished by the Jews themselves. And that is why we open chapter 5 with what one writer has called "a shock of pain."

It has been said that in a church quarrel the devil remains neutral and supplies ammunition to both sides.

On a North Dakota prairie, an abandoned church is being ravaged by the elements. Broken windows and sagging front steps overshadow memories of the days when the building was crowded for Sunday services. While the church was engaged in a fruitful ministry in the community, division crept in. It began when hard feelings developed between two leading families and then spread to the entire congregation as sides were quickly taken. Soon attendance began to decline and in a few short years the congregation sold the property and disbanded. The rotting timbers are a stern reminder of the destructive power of internal strife (D. McCarthy, "Disabled by Discord," *Sunday School Times and Gospel Herald*, April 1973, p. 15).

Abraham was sensitive to the dangers of internal strife. Genesis 13 tells the story of the range war that broke out between the cowboys of Abraham's cattle and those of Lot's cattle. Abraham saw immediately that such strife could not be tolerated, especially because "the Canaanite and the Perizzite dwelled then in the land" (v. 7). It was a scandal, and one that threatened to dishonor the God Abraham was known to worship.

The New Testament writers solemnly warned against strife among believers. James wrote, "Where envying and strife is, there is confusion and every evil work" (James 3:16). Paul cautioned the Galatians, "If ye bite and devour one another, take heed that ye be not consumed one of another" (Gal. 5:15).

Just after effective measures were adopted to thwart the enemies of the Jews, Nehemiah was faced with the potentially destructive influence of internal strife.

The Complaint of the Poor (5:1-5)

Nehemiah had been appointed governor, a fact mentioned in this chapter for the first time (v. 14). No doubt the weight of that office became particularly heavy as he was forced to listen to the strident cries of the complaining poor, at a time when there was much work yet to be finished on the wall and when the enemy was still lurking outside the gates.

But the poor had a strong case against their rich brethren—and it centered around the familiar social and economic problems of hunger, debts, and taxes.

Representatives of three distinct groups pressed their cases with the governor. The first to be heard were laborers who, having large families, were in urgent need of food (v. 2). These people did not even own property against which to borrow money. Their meager resources were used up while they worked on the wall; and in the language of desperation they said, in effect, "If we are not given grain, we'll take it rather than see our families die of starvation."

Another group to speak consisted of those who owned a little property but who were compelled to mortgage it in order to purchase food (v. 3). The famine was caused by a reduction of workers on the land while the wall-building was in progress and also by the near presence of the enemy, which interfered with agriculture outside Jerusalem. There is a note of desperation here as well, for the Jews had a strong attachment to family property and would sell or mortgage it only if survival was at stake.

The third group complained about the burdensome tax imposed by the Persian king. Borrowing money to pay their tax by pledging their crops, they were unable to repay their creditors, lost their fields and vineyards, and were even forced to sell their children into slavery (vv. 4-5). Reduced to the point of despair, they laid the matter before Nehemiah. "Why should the rich profit from the trouble that has fallen upon all of us, especially since they are our brethren?"

After the Civil War, the South was visited by many "carpet-baggers," traveling men usually from the North, who tried to make fortunes by taking advantage of the region's unsettled conditions. Profiteers invariably cluster round emergencies and disasters like vultures hovering over a carcass.

But should it have happened in ancient Israel? It was just such violations of social justice by the wealthy with respect to their poorer neighbors that the pre-exilic prophets had denounced. They declared that such sins were certain to bring on Israel's punishment (see Isa. 5:8; Amos 2:8; 4:1; 5:11; Micah 2:2; Hab. 2:6-7). How little the Children of Israel had learned from exile!

In this situation Nehemiah faced the most severe test of his leadership. How would he cope with this crisis? What measures would he take?

The Condemnation of the Nobles (5: 6-13)

Columnist Louis Cassels has said that the hardest moral duty of our time is for men and women to keep on caring. We are exposed daily to so much human tragedy that we experience what someone has called "compassion fatigue." Having felt sorry for so many flood victims, earthquake victims, and war victims, we simply cannot muster the sympathy we know we ought to have for fresh casualties. But even worse than compassion fatigue, said Cassels, is "indignation fatigue." "Many of us seem to have lost the capacity to get mad—or at least, as mad as we ought to get about lying, cheating, and stealing . . . To be indifferent to wrongdoing, to shrug it off or laugh at it, is a symptom of advanced degradation of the moral sense. Someone seems to have administered a massive dose of novocaine to our national conscience" (*The Dallas Morning News*, September 27, 1972).

Nehemiah was not afflicted with compassion fatigue or indignation fatigue. He records his response to the outcry of the oppressed, "And I was very angry when I heard their cry and these words" (v. 6). What the ridicule of the enemies had failed to do, the injustices of the rich Jews accomplished. The opposition from pagans was expected but not this disruption from his own countrymen—and the governor was incensed, as were Wilberforce, who centuries later was angry against the gross evils of slavery in the British Empire, and Lord Shaftesbury, who was indignant over the exploitation of women and children in factories and mines. Nehemiah handled his anger in the right way, as is seen in the developments that follow.

According to verse 7, Nehemiah did three things. First, he consulted with himself or "reflected upon the matter" (v. 7a, BERK). Nehemiah knew the wisdom of deliberating before taking action. Hasty reactions and snap judgments only intensify problems. By giving himself time to analyze and evaluate the situation, Nehemiah avoided rash actions that could have further deteriorated the relationships involved. It also enabled him to see the justice of the complaint. Nehemiah thus stands in great contrast to Rehoboam, who listened to the complaints of his tax-burdened subjects but refused to grant relief and instead made their burdens heavier. Small wonder that as a result they rebelled and left Rehoboam with only a small portion of the kingdom (1 Kings 12).

Next, Nehemiah confronted the nobles (v. 7b). He did not allow the problems to smolder indefinitely but courageously faced and rebuked the guilty parties. One writer states, "It was no little bravery in Nehemiah to face these tigers of his own nation, while guarding Jerusalem from the foreign foe." Did he think twice before approaching these influential nobles and rulers? Could he risk losing their support when the job of rebuilding was only half done?

Nehemiah determinedly faced these "tigers" knowing that he must do what was right, letting the chips fall where they may. It appears that he had a private conference with them first, rebuking them for lending money at exorbitant interest. In fact, according to the Mosaic Law, interest was not to be charged on loans to poor fellow Israelites (see Ex. 22:25; Lev. 25:35-37; Deut. 23:19-20).

The private conference had no effect on the nobles and rulers, so Nehemiah brought the matter before a "great assembly" (v. 7c). While such a gathering had no special legal authority, the full pressure of public opinion might be brought to bear against the leaders.

In the presence of all the people, Nehemiah revealed the fact that in the Exile he had redeemed Jews sold into slavery to their heathen neighbors. Yet in Jerusalem, the opposite was happening —Jews were selling their brethren into bondage. Were they planning to continue this shocking practice? Too ashamed to reply, the nobles hung their heads in silence (v. 8).

Next, Nehemiah directly charged them with moral wrongdoing (v. 9). And he appealed to them to consider their testimony before the surrounding nations. Divisive practices do tarnish the testimony of God's people. Thus, Paul exhorted the Colossian Christians, "Walk in wisdom toward them that are without" (Col. 4:5).

Wrote one author, "Christianity has shown that it is incapable of meeting present problems. It has failed because those who claim the Christian faith do not live up to its principles."

But many do live according to Christian principles. An evangelist holding meetings in a certain city boarded a bus and bought some tokens. When he got to his seat he noticed that he had been given too much change. He returned it to the conductor who said, "I've been listening to you preach all week and I gave you too much change purposely to see if you would live up to your own sermons!"

Nehemiah then startled the listening crowd with the frank admission that he had found his own family engaged in the oppression (v. 10, NASB), and he accepted full responsibility.

A leader must not only expose problems; he must also provide solutions. Nehemiah knew that according to the Law, the Jews could not expect God to bless them if they continued to disobey in these matters (see Deut. 23:20). He firmly though graciously requested the nobles (1) to cease lending money for profit and (2) to give back the lands and houses on which they had foreclosed as well as the interest they had collected (v. 11).

The reluctant nobles accepted the proposals with a verbal statement (v. 12a), but Nehemiah was realistic enough to know they might break their promise later when they were away from the angry assembly. He therefore required a stronger form of commitment. The priests administered solemn oaths to the nobles (v. 12b) and Nehemiah shook out the front of his robe, dramatizing what God would do to the person who violated his oath—he would be shaken loose from his things and be empty (v. 13).

The great assembly closed with all the people praising God that the problems had been resolved under Nehemiah's wise leadership. He had a firm grasp of the principle that no nation can hope for survival against its external foes if it has not first purged itself from corruption within. History has repeatedly proved Nehemiah right.

The Conduct of Nehemiah (5:14-19)

Nehemiah's dealings with the greedy moneylenders led him to catalog in a guileless manner the praiseworthy financial policies of his entire administration. It is apparent that these opening chapters of the book were written at the close of his first term of 12 years and this immediate material was not included in his remarks to the selfish nobles.

Nehemiah made it clear that during his 12-year administration (444-432 B.C.), neither he nor his household demanded their rightful salaries from the people (v. 14). During his entire tenure Nehemiah provided for the expenses of his official position out of his own purse. This was in spite of the fact that his predecessors in office had depended on the usual public assessment to support their bureaucracy (v. 15). It should not be assumed that Nehemiah condemned the previous governors for their practice. Rather, he simply waived his own right and this made him free to speak out openly against the greediness of others.

In this action Nehemiah reminds us of Paul, who argued vigorously in 1 Corinthians 9 for his rights as an apostle, and then declared, "Nevertheless we did not use this right, but we endure all things, that we may cause no hindrance to the Gospel of Christ" (1 Cor. 9:12, NASB). And Nehemiah said concerning his right to the governor's salary, "But so did not I, because of the fear of God" (v. 15b).

For the love of God and His work, Paul and Nehemiah were willing to relinquish their rights. In both cases, it was strictly a personal matter. Would many of us be willing to do the same, and for the same motivation?

Nehemiah next affirmed that during his administration, particularly during the time of the intense activity on the walls, neither he nor his household engaged in land speculation. The opportunity to make a profit from the distress of his brethren by buying their land at a low price was an ever-present temptation, but one that was steadfastly resisted (v. 16).

What major city has escaped its share of land scandals? Unscrupulous politicians knowing of future development plans for airports, highways, and commercial centers have often purchased land for the sole purpose of selling it back at huge profits. Nehemiah would have no part in such practice. He always operated above board.

Finally, Nehemiah gave another proof of his generosity as governor. At his own expense he regularly entertained over 150 officials, plus diplomatic visitors from outside Judah (v. 17). The daily provision, while not as ostentatious as Solomon's (see 1 Kings 4:22-23), was nonetheless costly, considering the poverty of the times (v. 18).

Nehemiah concluded his reflections on his own conduct as governor with the quaint prayer, "Remember me, O my God, for good, according to all that I have done for this people" (v. 19, NASB). This is, as one writer has said, "not a presumptuous conceit but a childlike simplicity." He knew the people would soon forget his sacrificial service and prayed that God would not. Ultimately, his goal was the approval of God, and he had done all of these things not to receive the praise of men but the rewards of God. The writer to the Hebrews assures us that it would be contrary to the character of God not to remember and reward such labors as those of Nehemiah, "For God is not unrighteous to forget your work and labor of love, which ye have showed toward His name, in that ye have ministered to the saints, and do minister" (Heb. 6:10).

It has been said that the true character of a man is revealed in a time of crisis, and that is doubly true if the man occupies a leadership position. Certainly, Nehemiah's true character as a leader is reflected by the manner in which he met this severe challenge; in the process, he demonstrated once again many vital qualities of leadership. It is clear that he possessed:

1. Capacity for moral indignation
2. Compassion for the oppressed
3. Concern for social justice
4. Courage to denounce evil, even when rich and influential men were involved
5. Consciousness of the fact that he labored for the approval of God and not men.

A young man once studied violin under a world-renowned master. Eventually, the time came for his first recital. Following each selection, despite the cheers of the crowd, the performer seemed dissatisfied. Even after the last number, with the shouts louder than ever, the talented violinist stood watching an elderly man in the balcony. Finally, the elderly one smiled and nodded in approval. Immediately, the young man relaxed and beamed with happiness. The applause of the crowd had meant nothing to him till he had first won the hearty approval of his famous teacher.

The Christian also must serve for God's approval, for in that he is rewarded.

6
A War of Nerves

Calvin Coolidge was once asked how he managed to remain calm when surrounded by troubles on every side. He answered, "Oh, I never let trouble bother me, for I have discovered that if you see ten troubles coming down the road toward you, you need not be frightened, because before they get to you, nine of them will go into the ditch, and the other one will probably be so weak by the time it reaches you that you can handle it easily."

Problems continued to plague Nehemiah and with God's help he successfully coped with each one. After dealing with internal difficulties caused by economic and social inequities, he was forced to face the renewed attacks of his enemies who now launched their final drive to halt construction.

Open opposition in the forms of mockery and threats had totally failed. Power politics had been ineffective. The work had advanced with remarkable speed in spite of the temporary delay caused by internal dissension among the Jews. The antagonists saw, therefore, that they must change their tactics and as one writer stated, "they turned from force to fraud." They launched a war of nerves on Nehemiah because they had at last come to see that he was the key to the entire project—remove him from the scene and the work would immediately cease. Accordingly, the enemies resorted to the tactics of intrigue, slander, treachery, and subversion to achieve their purpose of disrupting the work of the Jews.

Opposition by Intrigue (6:1-4)

The problem (vv. 1-2). Word reached Sanballat and his fellow conspirators (from spies inside Jerusalem?) that final repairs to the wall had been completed but that the doors had not yet been set in their sockets. Alarmed by this news, the enemies sent a message to Nehemiah, "Come, let us meet together in some one of the villages in the plain of Ono" (v. 2). The invitation was to attend a summit conference of sorts, in a neutral location near Joppa, between Ashdod and Samaria and outside the borders of Judah. Their plausible purpose seemed to be to plan for a peaceful coexistence, to resolve their differences so that all parties involved could live together in mutual understanding. But there was a hidden agenda. The real purpose of the proposed conference was to lure Nehemiah away from Jerusalem to where his assassination would be easier. With this dynamic leader off the scene, the morale of the Jews would sag, the work would stop, and the enemies would gain control.

But Nehemiah was not taken in by this confidence game. He recognized immediately that they had only one purpose in mind, and that was to do him harm.

John Huss, a Bohemian Reformer, and William Tyndale, an English Reformer, both had experiences similar to Nehemiah's, but with tragic ends. Huss was invited to attend the Council of Constance in 1414 to answer charges against him, and was promised safe conduct both ways by the emperor. In less than a month, however, he was seized and thrown in a dungeon, later to be condemned by the Council and burned at the state in the year 1415. Tyndale, the English Bible translator, was living in exile in Belgium when he was invited to have lunch with a supposed friend. It turned out to be a trap. Tyndale was arrested and several months later, in 1535, was strangled and burned.

The response (vv. 3-4). Nehemiah's reply to the invitation was simple and terse, "I am doing a great work, so that I cannot come down; why should the work cease, while I leave it, and come down to you?" (v. 3) With Nehemiah it was a matter of principle. The work on the walls was God's appointment for him at this time and to leave it even temporarily to pursue something else would be to forsake his first priority. Whatever God has called *us* to do, let us beware of being sidetracked by fruitless side issues. The Lord's work is a serious obligation and not something to be laid down and taken up at will.

The desperation to which Sanballat and his accomplices were driven is indicated by the fact that the letters of invitation came four times to Nehemiah, each one doubtless becoming more urgent (v. 4). This was a subtle trick of Satan and while it had succeeded with Balaam (Num. 22) and Samson (Judges 16), Nehemiah did not fall for it.

A volume published in Israel tells the story of biblical events in the form of a modern daily newspaper. Following is the news-story relating how Nehemiah handled the plot of the enemy:

Nehemiah Again Puts Off
'Big 4' Meeting at Ono
Special to CHRONICLES

Shechem, 25 Tishri. From Samaritan sources it is learned that Governor Nehemiah of Judah has again turned down the invitation of Sanballat, head of the district of Samaria, to come to the village of Ono, on the Judah-Samaria border, for a conference of the "Big Four" of the area: Gashmu, leader of the Edomites, Tobiah, leader of the Ammonites, Sanballat, and Nehemiah.

Sanballat issued an announcement today in which he sharply criticized Nehemiah for his repeated refusal to appear at such a meeting—the purpose of which, according to Sanballat, is "simply to adjust the relations among these rulers and bring about peace in the area."

Fourth Call

The Samaritan leader claims that this is the fourth time that Nehemiah has asked for a postponement of the conference on the grounds that he is too busy. This despite the fact that Ono, the place designated as the site of the meeting, is no more than four and one-half hours' ride from Jerusalem.

"The responsibility for anything that may happen and for the blood that may be shed rests solely upon Nehemiah," the announcement concludes. (*Chronicles; News of the Past.* Jerusalem: The Reuboni Foundation).

Opposition by Slander (6: 5-9)

The problem (vv. 5-7). Another scheme was employed to incrimi-
nate Nehemiah. The enemy tried to discredit him by creating a
scandal. An open letter, written on leather or papyrus and left
unsealed so that its message would become public, was sent to
Nehemiah by Sanballat. The letter contained three charges: (1)
that Nehemiah and the Jews were plotting treason. Specifically, the
accusation was made that the work of fortifying the city was
carried on with the goal of rebelling against the Persian government (v. 6). (2) It was insinuated that Nehemiah had pretensions
to the throne, namely, that his real motive in all of this building
program was to become king in Jerusalem (6b). (3) Nehemiah
was charged with bribing some enthusiastic prophets to support
him in his quest for kingship (v. 7). There may have been some
misguided prophets in Jerusalem who thought the messianic age
had indeed come and that Nehemiah would be king, but it is un-
thinkable to believe that Nehemiah had anything to do with them.

Threatening to forward the information in this open letter to
the king of Persia, Sanballat subtly suggested, "Come now, therefore, and let us take counsel together" (v. 7b). This was black-
mail. Would Nehemiah capitulate and meet with the enemy?

The response (vv. 8-9). Nehemiah sent his answer by return
mail, indignantly repudiating the charges. After all, he had the
official support of King Artaxerxes whose letters of certification
he had brought to Jerusalem (see 2:9). Indeed, the whole story
was a fabrication of the sender, invented by evil minds for the
purpose of demoralizing the Jews so that the work on the walls
and gates would stop short of completion (v. 9).

But what if Artexerxes were persuaded to believe the charges of
treason? What if his mind were poisoned by the lying tongues of
the enemies of Jerusalem? Outwardly, Nehemiah was unwavering
and resolute. Inwardly, he sensed the gravity of the situation and
trembled. For this reason he fervently prayed, "Now therefore, O
God, strengthen my hands" (v. 9b).

How should we respond to slander? Following Nehemiah's example, a simple denial and prayer are sufficient. David wrote, "For
I have heard the slander of many; fear was on every side; while
they took counsel together against me, they devised to take away
my life. But I trusted in Thee, O Lord; I said, 'Thou art my

God. . . .' Let the lying lips be put to silence, which speak
grievous things proudly and contemptuously against the righteous"
(Ps. 31:13-14, 18).

Christians should avoid becoming tools in Satan's hands by
maligning or slandering another. In such a situation, the damage
is often irrevocable.

The story is told of a peasant who slandered a friend. On
discovering that what he had said was untrue, he went to the
village priest for help. The priest told him to take a bag of
feathers and to place one feather on each doorstep of his community. This he did, and returned to the priest, announcing that
he had completed the penance for his sin. But the priest sternly
ordered him to take his bag and pick up each feather he had
dropped. When the man replied that by this time the wind had
blown the feathers away and they were irrecoverable, the priest
reminded him that words are like feathers: once they are dropped,
and that easily, it is impossible to get them back.

Opposition by Treachery (6:10-14)

The problem (v. 10). Attempts to lure Nehemiah outside the walls
had failed. The adversaries, therefore, used their inside connections to launch an attack on the governor. Their tool was Shemaiah, both a prophet and a priest who apparently invited
Nehemiah to visit him in his home where he was confined. As a
supposed friend, he pretended because of this to be in great
personal danger and kept himself in seclusion. But this meant,
of course, that Nehemiah too was in danger and should seek a
hiding place. Shemaiah declared to Nehemiah, as if by the spirit
of prophecy, that his enemies planned to assassinate him and
proposed that they flee together to the temple where they could
shut the doors and be safe. The suggestion was a shocking one,
because though it was legitimate for an Israelite to seek refuge
at the brazen altar outside the temple proper (cf. Ex. 21:13-14),
Shemaiah proposed they enter the Holy Place, where only priests
could go, and there hide from the assassins.

The response (vv. 11-14). Nehemiah indignantly rejected the
scheme of Shemaiah, and for two reasons. First, as governor he
was responsible for the protection of the people. Should he, holding the highest position in the state, display cowardice and betray

his countrymen by running to hide? (v. 11a) At all hazards he would remain at his post.

Furthermore, Nehemiah knew that, according to the Scriptures, a lay-Israelite was forbidden to enter the Holy Place under penalty of death (see Num. 18:7). He asked, "Should a man like me flee? And could one such as I go into the temple to save his life? I will not go in" (v. 11, NASB).

The whole thing was a treacherous plot, another veiled attempt on his life. And Nehemiah had enough perception to know that the trap had been hatched by Tobiah and Sanballat with the evil counsel of some unscrupulous prophets and Noadiah (vv. 12, 14).

The unpleasant encounter with Shemaiah, however, left Nehemiah somewhat shaken. Acutely aware of the strength and subtlety of the enemy and of his own human weakness, he prayed that God would deal with his foes (v. 14). Thus Nehemiah rested his case with God, confident that He would judge the opponents of the work and vindicate His servant.

For Nehemiah, the issue was clear and simple. The Word of God had spoken and for him to violate the sanctity of the temple would be to disobey the Scriptures and that would be sin (v. 13). Tragically, many in our society no longer regard the Scriptures as authoritative in matters of religion and morals. Says one writer:

When moral dilemmas arise, the reaction of those who have rejected absolutes is pathetic. University professors ask their students not to cheat even though they cannot tell them why they shouldn't. Or if they do, the reasons are usually trivial; such as, "You will fail"; or "It's important that you learn to do research." Parents don't want their children to participate in sex orgies, but when their children ask why, the best they can do is plead, "Think of what our friends will say. You are ruining our reputation." But if the child does not care whether he knows how to do research and cares even less about what the friends of the family think, he has no reason to follow traditional moral codes. The fault lies not merely with the children, but with the older generation that looks with nostalgia to the days when moral values were highly regarded, although they have lost the basis of values they had inherited. Francis Schaeffer tells the story of John Gard-

ner, head of the Urban Coalition, who gave a lecture on
restoring values to our culture. When he was asked on what
he based his values, he could only look down and say, "I
do not know" (Erwin W. Lutzer, *The Morality Gap.* [Chicago: Moody Press, 1972] p. 116).

Nehemiah based his values, and therefore his actions, on the
absolutes of the Word of God.

Opposition by Subversion (6:15-19)
"So the wall was finished"—and in an amazing 52 days. Some
have suggested that this time frame was too short and have
adopted the speculative notion of Josephus that it took two years
and four months to complete the work. But there is no reason
whatever to amend the text. The longer time would be entirely
out of keeping with the context which describes a situation of
haste and urgency. Likewise, it should be remembered that large
numbers of people were involved in the project and that large
portions of the walls only required repair and not complete rebuilding. Further, the building materials were readily accessible,
the workers were well organized, Nehemiah gave everyone steady
encouragement, and the Jews enjoyed the special favor of God
in their endeavor.

The effect on the Jews of the completion of the walls is not
noted at this point. Nehemiah observed, no doubt with great
satisfaction, that a feeling of discouragement now passed over to
the enemy. They were "much cast down in their own eyes: for
they perceived that this work was wrought of our God" (v. 16).
The adversaries concluded that the complete frustration of all of
their methods of opposition could only be accounted for by the
intervention of the God of Israel. "Then said they among the
heathen, 'The Lord hath done great things for them' " (Ps. 126:2).

Lest the people and their leaders place their confidence in the
finished walls of Jerusalem rather than in the God of Jerusalem,
Nehemiah added a postscript to remind everyone that the dangers
were not over even though the walls were up. A treasonable
correspondence was being carried on between Tobiah and some
disloyal Jewish nobles (v. 17). Furthermore, Tobiah and his son
had married Jewish women (v. 18). Tobiah used these family

connections to his own advantage to aid his continuing purpose of subverting Nehemiah's influence. The Jewish in-laws of Tobiah sang his praises to Nehemiah and then relayed back to him everything they learned from the governor. Based on this information, Tobiah wrote threatening letters to Nehemiah, perhaps of the same nature as the open letter previously sent by Sanballat (see vv. 6-7).

"The stoutest walls will not protect from treason within the ramparts. So after all the labor of completing the fortifications Nehemiah's trust must still be in God above" (W. F. Adeney, *Ezra, Nehemiah & Esther*, p. 270).

The continued pressures of the enemy must not be allowed to distract us from Nehemiah's incredible accomplishments. He was a man with a sense of mission and though the enemies kept hammering away at him, he persisted in the work till it was finished.

Our youngest son, Jon, is now a collegiate varsity football player. His football career began with the YMCA when he was in the third grade. During the second game, the coach frowned at him and he decided to quit. All through the season he watched his little friends play football and he couldn't participate. Soon there appeared a small sign on his bulletin board. It is still there. Scrawled in his handwriting are the words, "Quitters never win and winners never quit."

In the work of God, it is always too soon to quit. That was Nehemiah's watchword and should be ours also.

"Therefore, my beloved brethren, be ye steadfast, unmovable, always abounding in the work of the Lord, forasmuch as ye know that your labor is not in vain in the Lord" (1 Cor. 15:58).

7

Roots

Once, when Winston Churchill was young, he had lunch with the Chancellor of the Exchequer who said to him, "My dear Winston, the experiences of a long life have convinced me that nothing ever happens." Churchill, on the other hand was to learn in his long lifetime that nearly everything happens, even things considered impossible. So stated a *Time* magazine essay which continued,

Anwar Sadat's trip to Jerusalem, and all that has followed from it, suggests again the ingenuity with which some men and women have approached the seemingly insoluble problem, the historical impossibility. Old impregnable conundrums usually fall to the simplest, most elegant assaults. Alexander's sword at one stroke solved all the mystification of the Gordian knot. Hannibal crossed the Alps with elephants—military genius riding through the snow upon absurdity. Gandhi defeated the British raj with a contradiction: nonviolent resistance. In 1955 a weary black woman in Montgomery, Alabama, Rosa Parks, refused to surrender her seat on a bus to a white man; at that instant, three centuries of America's racial tragedy began slowly to unravel (*Time*, January 9, 1978, p. 74).

Nehemiah clearly possessed this kind of genius. Jerusalem exhibited an "old impregnable conundrum" for almost 150 years

—the walls lay in hopeless ruins. But Nehemiah assaulted the problems and the "historical impossibility" was dissolved.

Yet, though the walls had been restored, Nehemiah did not consider his work to be at an end. His deep concern now was for people, for they too needed restoration. Chapter 7 serves as a pivot that moves us from the discussion of the restoration of the walls (chapters 1—6) to the restoration of the people (chapters 8—13). Two things confront us in this chapter: a description of security measures for Jerusalem, and a register of the remnant that returned from Persia.

Safeguarding the City, 7:1-3

Apparently, Nehemiah remembered from history that despite its great walls Babylon had fallen to Persia for lack of watchfulness. Determined that it would not happen to Jerusalem, he set in motion several measures of defense. The times were still precarious with the dangers of possible attack from the outside and probable intrigue of traitors on the inside.

Nehemiah first assigned the temple guards (porters) as sentinels to watch the entire city, and augumented their force by adding singers and Levites (v. 1). He next appointed two municipal officers, Hanani and Hananiah, to take charge of Jerusalem's security. The former, one of the Jews who had brought word to Nehemiah in Persia of the plight of his people in Jerusalem, (see 1:2), was clearly a man of great courage and one who inspired the confidence of his countrymen. Hananiah was the officer in charge of the temple fortress, a man of experience in security matters. It is said of him that "he was a faithful man, and feared God above many" (v. 2). The new leaders of Jerusalem were men of excellent qualifications and this was another tribute to Nehemiah's leadership ability—he knew how to pick good men for vital tasks.

As a further precaution, Nehemiah ordered that the gates of Jerusalem were not to be opened till the sun was high in the heavens (v. 3a). Customarily, the gates were swung open at sunrise, but his safety measure would prevent enemies from gaining the advantage of a surprise attack by entering the city before the inhabitants were up and about.

It must be emphasized that gates were absolutely crucial to the defense of ancient cities. Made of wood and bronze, they were often bound with heavy copper bands or sheathed in copper plates. Towers were sometimes built at the gates so that defenders could throw boiling pitch or oil on the enemy. Bolts made the gates secure when closed (see Neh. 7:3). Until the battering ram was perfected, gates were the only places successful assaults could be made against a walled city. Nehemiah was fully aware of this fact and concentrated on their repair and on the control of traffic through them.

Nehemiah directed that the citizens were to be organized as a home guard or civilian defense corps to take turns standing guard at night outside their own homes (v. 3b). This was a shrewd move since it assured they would be more alert when their own homes were involved.

Watchfulness was the essential element of protection against the enemy. An interesting parallel is found in Paul's instruction to New Testament believers who also faced an enemy, though not a human foe: "For we wrestle not against flesh and blood, but against principalities, against powers, against the rulers of darkness of this world, against spiritual wickedness in high places" (Eph. 6:12). The same danger is real for us because we are surrounded by the enemy. We are urged to accept and put on the "whole armor of God," namely, the panoply which God provides, so that we can resist and be victorious in the evil day when Satan attacks. As we take up the individual pieces of the armor (see Eph. 6:14-17), we are to do so in a spirit of prayer and watchfulness: "Praying always . . . and watching thereunto with all perseverance" (Eph. 6:18).

The message sent through the Apostle John to the church at Sardis also emphasized watchfulness (see Rev. 3:2-3). The church there heard the warning with memory of the lessons of history, for Sardis was captured by the Persian King Cyrus in a striking way. The Greek historian Herodotus informs us that from her position Sardis was considered nearly impregnable. Behind her rose Mount Tmolus; from that mountain there went out a narrow ridge of rock like a pier, and on that ridge the citadel of Sardis was built. Cyrus besieged Sardis, and wished to capture it with all speed, for he could not advance till Sardis fell. He sent a message to his troops that there would be a special reward for any man who worked out a method whereby the cliff could be scaled and the fortress taken. Hyeroeades, a Mardian soldier, studied the cliffs to figure out a way of storming them. He saw a Lydian soldier on the battlements and, as he watched, the Lydian accidentally dropped his helmet over the walls, down the cliff. Hyeroeades saw this Lydian mount the battlements, pick his way down the cliffs, recover his helmet, and climb back. He carefully marked in his mind the way the Lydian soldier had taken, and that night led a picked band of troops up the cliffs. When they reached the top, they found the defenses completely unguarded. The garrison never dreamed anyone could find a way up the cliffs and felt themselves completely safe. So Hyeroeades and his comrades entered in unopposed, and Sardis was taken.

The Lord warned that just as the city of Sardis was lost for failure to be alert and watchful, so the church there could be lost by taking its safety for granted. In fact, Christ's complaint was that while they appeared outwardly to be alive they were in reality dead (Rev. 3:1). Their praying was only a formal and empty pretense, their singing was correct but devoid of true worship, and their giving deteriorated to a mere fulfillment of duty. Everything was form and ritual, mechanical and meaningless. They were charged, therefore, to be watchful and to strengthen what remained. The paralysis of complacency, the disease of heresy, the violence of persecution—these dangers and more threaten the individual believer and the local church in every generation. We must always be vigilant and watchful.

A soldier was once posted in a forest to watch for the approach of Indians. It was a position of extreme danger, three different men having been surprised and killed at this post without having had time to fire a shot. In a short while, the soldier observed an object moving among the trees. He leveled his rifle till it came nearer and he saw it was a wild hog. Another object came in sight —it was the same thing. Presently, in another direction leaves rustled and a third hog appeared. The soldier thought he observed a slight awkwardness in the movements of this one and felt it might possibly be an Indian covered with a hog skin. He raised his rifle and fired. With a bound and a yell the Indian leaped to his feet and fell back dead. The man saved his life with his watchfulness and prevented a surprise attack on the garrison. This is what Nehemiah sought to provide for the protection of Jerusalem.

Surveying the People, 7: 4-73

Still not satisfied, Nehemiah continued to think about the welfare of Jerusalem. He contemplated the large empty areas within the walls and wondered how they could best be filled with people. After all, the city was now a safe place to live and offered certain advantages over the small villages scattered over the countryside. A larger population would cause the capital to prosper and would strengthen its defenses.

As he thought and prayed on the matter he felt led of God to take a census of the people (v. 5). In this way, he could discover population patterns in the towns and countryside and determine which districts could best afford to lose a portion of their inhabitants to Jerusalem.

The census, in accord with Jewish practice, was to be genealogical, that is, according to family and tribal relationships (see Num. 1:17-47; 1 Chron. 21:5-6). In the course of this preparation, while perhaps looking through the temple archives for precedents, Nehemiah discovered the "register of the genealogy of them which came up at the first" (v. 5b). This newly discovered list recorded by families the names of the Jews who came from Persia to Palestine in 536 B.C. under the leadership of Zerubbabel. The same list with minor variations, is found in Ezra 2.

Who was included in the register? The leaders (v. 7); the people by families (vv. 8-25); the people by cities (vv. 26-38); the religious leaders including priests (vv. 39-42) and Levites together with singers and porters (vv. 43-45); the Nethinims or temple servants (vv. 46-56); descendants of Solomon's servants (vv. 57-60); and returnees without pure Jewish descent (vv. 61-65). The record is concluded with the total number of people (vv. 66-67), animals (vv. 68-69), and gifts given for the support of the work (vv. 70-72).

How can we account for the variations in the list as recorded in Ezra 2 and Nehemiah 7? Some Bible scholars have suggested that Ezra's list was compiled in Babylon some time prior to the departure whereas Nehemiah's was made in Jerusalem after the arrival of the exiles. It is suggested that people may have joined the company late, and not been listed, or dropped out at the last minute and their names retained, later to be dropped. Others may have started but not completed the arduous trip. One difficulty with this theory is that the sum total in each list is exactly the same (see Ezra 2:64 and Neh. 7:66). A better solution seems to be that the few differences in names and numbers on the two lists represent errors that did not exist in the original autographs but were made by the copyists who handed the material down from generation to generation.

Why should this list appear in the Scriptures twice? In Ezra 2, it stands in its original and proper historical context, giving a register of those who first returned to Jerusalem in 536 B.C. under Zerubbabel. Those people and their activities are described in Ezra 1—6. Since it was a genealogical or family census, Nehemiah found it useful a full century later (in 444 B.C.) and included it in his memoirs as the basis for his program of encouraging some to move to Jerusalem.

But there is a deeper reason for the double inclusion of the list. Jewish people historically revered their genealogies because the records gave them a personal and national identity, reminding them who they were. Nehemiah's fellow Jews in particular might well have experienced an identity crisis. They needed this compelling reminder of the past and of their linkage to it, for they were a part of the people of God who had been removed from the land for sin and restored in grace to fulfill the divine purpose. But would they see their present and future obligation in the light of their heritage? This is the main burden of the rest of the Book of Nehemiah.

What is the abiding truth of Nehemiah 7? Paul assured us that all Scripture is both inspired and profitable (2 Tim. 3:16). We may properly ask, therefore, what is the profit of this chapter? Surely there is an analogy to be drawn between this genealogy and the Christian's spiritual pedigree. The importance of the post-exilic Jews being able to prove the purity of their ancestry was underscored by the fact that some who could not were removed from the priesthood (Neh. 7:63-65). But can the Christian be sure of his spiritual family history? The New Testament clearly affirms that the one who receives Christ as Saviour is born into the family of God (see John 1:12). As a child of God he partakes of the divine nature and his eternal destiny is fixed.

Since the publication of Alex Haley's bestseller, *Roots*, interest in family genealogies has grown rapidly. (I confess to having ordered a volume on the Campbell family history from a genealogical research institute.) Certainly, this may give a person some sense of belonging, of connection with history, of identity. Yet, it is in being a member of God's family that a person finds the greatest fulfillment of these basic human needs. British author and clergyman John Stott explains that conversion "relates me to God, to man and to history. It enables me to answer the most basic of all human questions, 'Who am I?' and to say, 'In Christ I am a son of God. In Christ I am united to all the redeemed people of God, past, present, and future. In Christ I discover my identity. In Christ I find my feet. In Christ I come home' " (*The Message of Galatians* [London: InterVarsity Press, 1968], p. 102).

8

A Water Gate Revival

An African tribal chieftain was educated in English schools and was able to gain an audience with Queen Victoria. He asked her, "To what do you attribute the great prosperity of the British Empire?" To answer the question she picked up her Bible and said, "Take this Book and its message to your people and they will likewise prosper."

Daniel Webster of our own country also emphasized that the only solid basis for civilization was the Word of God. On the occasion of the completion of the Bunker Hill Monument in Boston on June 17, 1843, Webster spoke of the coming of the Pilgrim Fathers to the new world: "They brought with them a full portion of all the riches of the past, in science, art, morals, religion and literature. The Bible came with them. And it is not to be doubted that to the free and universal reading of the Bible is to be ascribed in that age, ascribed in every age, that men were much indebted for right views of civil liberty."

If the Jerusalem of Nehemiah was to remain strong and free, more was needed than city walls and security measures. A spiritual vacuum existed in the lives of the returned exiles. Their ignorance of the Law of God was appalling, and Nehemiah knew they could not handle physical battles well unless they were spiritually fit. In chapter 8, therefore, we see the leaders of Jerusalem reinforcing the stone walls with a foundation of spiritual values for the population.

Bible Reading at the Water Gate (8:1-4)

The time of the great assembly was the seventh month (7:73b). This was the feast month par excellence in ancient Israel. According to Leviticus 23, the seventh month (*Tishri* or September to October) was the time for the celebration of the Feast of Trumpets, Day of Atonement, and Feast of Tabernacles. It was also the month that the Ark of the Covenant was moved into the temple (2 Chron. 5:3-5), that times of mourning were held in the captivity (Zech. 7:5), and that the returnees under Zerubbabel offered burnt offerings in the blackened ruins of the temple (Ezra 3). While this gathering does not seem to have been connected with any regularly constituted occasion, it was fitting that it should occur in the sacred month when the hearts of the people were more spiritually sensitive.

The place of the assembly was "at the square which was in front of the Water Gate" (8:1, NASB). This is probably the same place as that referred to in Ezra 10:9 where the repentant men of Judah and Benjamin met, located presumably between the southeast precincts of the temple and the eastern wall. For the first time since the completion of the walls, the people were able to meet in a public place without fear of being molested.

The purpose of the meeting was to hear the Word of God. The initiative was with the people who, through their representatives, asked Ezra to bring out, possibly from the temple, the Law of Moses (v. 8b). Their hunger for the Scriptures was no doubt rekindled through a renewed awareness that while their national integrity was guaranteed by the completed walls, their distinctiveness as the people of God could only be preserved by obedience to the Torah.

The key figure of the gathering was Ezra, who had come to Jerusalem in 458 B.C. to teach in Israel the statutes and judgments of God's Law (Ezra 7:10). After having led the people in a religious reformation (Ezra 9—10), Ezra disappeared from view. While it is possible that his age made it impossible for him to do the hard manual labor involved in the building project, it seems more probable to suppose that he was recalled to Persia and only returned after the walls were finished. His reappearance was added incentive to the people to ask their former spiritual leader to read the Scriptures to them.

A mission board was interviewing a number of candidates. One of them told of his previous involvement in political activity as a precinct chairman. Sensing his frustration with politics, a friend invited him to a Bible class where he heard the Gospel and was saved. He went immediately to the pastor of the church where he belonged and where he taught a Sunday School class. "We need some Bible study and we need it in a hurry!" he exclaimed. The pastor replied, "You'll have to go to one of the local colleges. We don't have time for that here."

But when Ezra heard the people cry, "Bring the Book!", his response was immediate. He brought out the scroll of the Law, probably the entire Pentateuch, on this momentous day. The "first day of the seventh month" (v. 2) was the Jewish New Year, *Rosh Hashanah*. It was to be a day of Holy convocation (Lev. 23:24), and while it is uncertain whether the Jews at this time were mindful of this fact, it was a significant day to signal the beginning of a religious revival in Israel.

This great service was marked by several important features. First, it was for families (vv. 2-3). And this was not an isolated instance, for it was customary for women and children to be included on such solemn occasions (see Deut. 31:12; Josh. 8:35; 2 Kings 23:2). The Lord is always interested in the spiritual nurture of the entire family.

In the second place, we observe with some astonishment that the service lasted for some six hours, from sunrise till noon (v. 3). For the occasion, the Jews had erected a wooden platform large enough for Ezra and 13 others who were possibly heads of families and whose presence lent weight to the occasion (v. 4). Thus, the scroll and the reader were in clear view of the assembly, with Ezra reading till he was exhausted, whereupon another on the platform would relieve him.

It is noteworthy also that "the ears of all the people were attentive unto the book of the Law" (v. 3b). The people had arisen very early and listened patiently hour after hour to the reading of the Scripture. Many of them had not heard the Word of God for many years; some had probably not heard it at all. It was a spiritual feast for their hungry souls as they sat in rapt attention. No wonder a work of God would soon be accomplished in their midst. A New Testament parallel is found in that dramatic scene where Cornelius and his household said to Peter, "Now therefore are we all here present before God, to hear all things that are commanded thee of God" (Acts 10:33). And a significant work of grace followed.

A faculty colleague was invited to teach a Sunday School class in a liberal church. Asking the people to open their Bibles, he was astonished that no one had a Bible. Sensing the indifference of the class and the frustration of the visiting teacher, the class president jumped up and said he would look for some. He located the janitor and the two men went down to the basement, unlocked a closet and found stacks of Bibles. They took them out, blew the dust off, and distributed them to the class. Tragically, after the hour of Bible teaching, they were collected and carried back down to the basement where they were once again locked in the closet. Small wonder that church is a spiritual desert!

Revival at the Water Gate (8: 5-18)

It is doubtful that there has ever been a genuine revival without the Word of God having a large part in it. This was the case in the time of Josiah and of Hezekiah, revivalist kings of Judah. And it was the recovery of the Scriptures that produced the Reformation of the 16th century.

A native of India, writing to a friend about a revival they were having, exclaimed, "We are having a great rebible here!" Few would want to quarrel with that.

Six things characterized the spiritual revival of Nehemiah 8: reverence for Scripture, worship of God, comprehension of Scripture, remorse for sin, rejoicing in fellowship with God, and obedience to the Word of God.

Reverence for the Scripture (v. 5). As Ezra unrolled the scroll of the Torah, the people stood to their feet, signifying their reverence for the Word of God that was to be read. This gesture later became characteristic of the Jews in the synagogue services, and even today in some churches the congregation stands for the reading of the Scriptures.

It is touching to see such veneration for the Word of God. It was a day when scrolls of Scripture were not easily multiplied and few people therefore had direct access to them. Even in the Middle Ages, before the advent of the printing press and the stimulus of the Reformation, Bibles were chained to pillars in the parish churches of England. In order to hear the Word of God, people were forced to attend church and listen to the reading of a chained Bible. Today, we in the West may be inclined to take the Bible for granted. Millions of copies in many languages are printed and circulated around the world, yet they are still scarce in some countries.

Peter Deyneka, Jr. told of a Christian couple touring Russia. In one hotel they had a maid who implored them to give her the Gospel of John they had left out on a bedside table. She explained that she was a believer and that her Bible had been destroyed 30 years before in the German siege of Leningrad. The couple gladly gave the maid a small Russian Bible which she received with grateful thanks and then quickly left. The next morning the maid met the couple in the hall and said, "I had to see you. I must thank you again for the precious gift you gave me yesterday. For 30 years I have been praying for a Bible. I have had prayer and life is good when I pray, but now I have a Bible. Last night I stayed up most of the night to read it." Who, indeed, can measure the value and blessing of the Word of God?

Worship of God (v. 6). Just before reading the Law, Ezra led the people in prayer, perhaps with words similar to those found at the end of Psalm 135:

> Bless the Lord, O house of Israel;
> Bless the Lord, O house of Aaron;
> Bless the Lord, O house of Levi;
> Ye that fear the Lord, bless the Lord.
> Blessed be the Lord out of Zion,
> which dwelleth at Jerusalem.
> Praise Ye the Lord.

The response of the people was twofold. They said, " 'Amen, Amen,' with lifting up their hands," indicating their participation with Ezra in his remarkable prayer of worship. Then they "bowed their heads, and worshiped the Lord with their faces to the ground," showing their devotion and adoration for the Lord but also their willing submission to His authority. Their attitude was that of the Psalmist who said,

> O come, let us worship and bow down;
> let us kneel before the Lord our Maker.
> For He is our God, and we are the people
> of His pasture, and the sheep of His hand
> (Ps. 95:6-7).

Could any audience have been more prepared for the ministry of the Word of God?

Comprehension of the Scripture (vv. 7-8). A third factor characterizing this revival was that the people were brought to an understanding of Scripture. How was this accomplished? The answer is instructive. First, there was the public reading of the Law of God. This was followed by an exposition of the meaning of the text. The result of this gracious ministry was that the people understood the Scripture. Apparently, Ezra was assisted by the Levites who helped with the reading and then explained the text in smaller groups.

One writer stated that this meeting at the Water Gate "set the pattern for Protestant worship and its emphasis on the exposition of the Word."

Alexander Whyte, the famed Scottish preacher, spoke of such masters of pulpit exposition as Chrysostom, Augustine, Calvin, Matthew Henry, Thomas Goodwin, and Joseph Parker, and then declared:

> All those men laid out their pulpit life on Ezra's exact plan. That is to say, not so much preaching trite and hackneyed sermons, on trite and hackneyed texts, but reading in the Law of God consecutively, giving the sense, and causing the people to understand the reading . . . . It is a noble tradition and a perfect method; only to do it well demands very hard labor and very wide reading and very deep thinking, as well as an early and a life-long preparation of the preacher's heart. But he who sets to himself this noblest of all possible tasks, and perseveres to the end in it, ever learning in it, ever improving in it, ever adding to his treasures of exposition and illustration, ever putting himself into his lecture, and ever keeping himself out of it, he will never grow old, he will never become worked out, he will never weary out his peo-

ple, but he will to old age bring forth his fruit in his season, and his leaf will not wither" (*Bible Characters* [Edinburgh: Oliphants Ltd., n.d.] p. 219).

It was Dr. Carl Armerding, venerable Bible teacher and pulpit expositor, who stood in the foyer of the Moody Church of Chicago one Sunday morning after delivering the message. His sight of the people leaving was partially obscured by a large pillar, and he overheard one well-dressed lady say to her friend, "Well, I don't think he is such a great preacher. Why, all he did was explain the Bible!"

Ezra and his helpers were the first in a long line of expository preachers who explained the Bible. This method of preaching has been blessed by God down through the centuries and continues to be an effective instrument for bringing Christians to spiritual maturity. Topical and textual preaching may often be inspiring and helpful but the spiritual benefits do not compare with those resulting from a preaching ministry like Ezra's. Blessed indeed are the believers who are privileged to sit under expository preaching of the Scriptures.

Remorse for sin (v. 9). The reading, interpretation, and application of the Law struck a responsive chord in the hearts of the Jews. Never had they heard it expounded so effectively. And did not their history remind them pointedly of what happened to those who neglected God's commandments? Comparing their conduct to the standards of God's Word, it was quickly apparent to them how far short they had fallen.

Dr. B. B. Warfield, Princeton theologian of a previous generation, said, "The Bible is the Word of God in such a way that when the Bible speaks, God speaks." And these Jews heard God speaking through the exposition of His Word. They were convicted concerning their disobedience to it and expressed their contrition by open mourning and weeping.

Israel's reformer king, Josiah, had a similar reaction: "And it came to pass, when the king had heard the words of the book of the Law, that he rent his clothes" (2 Kings 22:11).

We are reminded of the words of the writer of the Epistle to the Hebrews, "For the Word of God is quick, and powerful, and sharper than any two-edged sword, piercing even to the dividing asunder of soul and spirit, and of the joints and marrow, and is a discerner of the thoughts and intents of the heart" (Heb. 4:12). We are assured by this verse (1) that God's Word is living—as God is; (2) that it is active and energetic; (3) that it cuts or lays bare any pretense; (4) that it penetrates to the innermost recesses of our spiritual being; (5) and that it is a judge or critic of our thoughts. It was all of this to those who listened with open minds and receptive hearts in the time of Nehemiah.

And that is precisely why some avoid the Bible. It convicts them of their sin.

George Bernard Shaw, the British playwright once had a Bible. Four years before he died in 1950 he sold it to auctioneers who in turn sold it for $50 after Shaw's death. One of the selling points was an inscription on the flyleaf by the playwright himself:

"Except as a curiosity, this book is a most undesirable possession. . . . I must get rid of it. I really cannot bear it in my house!"

Rejoicing in God's Fellowship (vv. 10-12). Though Ezra, Nehemiah, and the Levites were heartened to see signs of contrition, they proceeded to comfort and still the people, reminding them that "this day" was for joy and not sorrow, for a feast and not a fast. "This day" seems clearly to be a reference to the first day of the seventh month (v. 2), the day that ushered in a month of worship, and that marked also the time of the celebration of the Feast of Trumpets.

The Jews were instructed to celebrate the festival with eating, drinking, and sharing, mindful of the fact that "the joy of the Lord is your strength (or stronghold)." Israel's joy was based on her confidence in God's protection. Their gladness was proportionate to their faith in God's providential care. Declared the Psalmist, "He is their strength in the time of trouble" (Ps. 37:39). The person who rejoices in the Lord has a strong fortress from which he can ward off his adversaries.

The response of the people was one of ready obedience to the directions just given (v. 12a). With sins judged and forsaken, the Jews celebrated the festival, rejoicing in fellowship with one another and with God. The reason for their joyful spirit is said to be "because they had understood the words that were declared unto them" (v. 12b). They had sorrowed because they had not kept the Law (v. 9), and now they rejoiced because they could understand it. Said one writer, "True joy is based on knowledge of and submission to God's Word. *This* is the joy of the Lord!"

Only the people of God can know true joy—in spite of the circumstances of life. Cyprian, a Christian martyr of the third century, wrote in a letter:

> This seems to be a cheerful world, Donatus, when I view it from the fair garden, under the shadow of these vines. But if I climbed some great mountain and looked out over the wide lands, you know very well what I would see. Great armies on the high roads; pirates on the seas; in the amphitheater, men murdered to please the applauding crowds; under all roofs, misery and selfishness. It is really a bad world, Donatus, an incredibly bad world. Yet in the midst of it I have found a quiet and holy people. They have discovered a joy which is a thousand times better than any pleasure in this single life. They are despised and persecuted, but they care not. They have overcome the world. These people are the Christians, and I am one of them.

Obedience to the Word of God (vv. 13-18). The great Bible reading that took place on the first day of the seventh month was only a beginning. Though the mass of people returned to their homes and towns, the heads of families, the priests, and Levites came back to Ezra on the second day to hear more (v. 13). By this time, the reading had progressed to Leviticus 23 and the people were reminded that on the 15th through the 22nd days of the seventh month they were to observe the Feast of Tabernacles (*Succoth*) by dwelling in booths (vv. 14-15).

This feast was the final fall harvest festival and the dwelling in booths was to remind the Jews of the temporary dwellings their fathers had in the wilderness. Many Jews of today still build such huts in their yards or on porches, decorating them with tree boughs and fall fruits to remind them of harvest.

Since this was one of the three appointed seasons when all able-bodied males in Israel were to appear at the temple in Jerusalem, it was considered a very sacred occasion. Josephus called it "the holiest and greatest of the Hebrew feasts." During this feast, water from the Pool of Siloam was poured out in ritual at the temple and Jesus chose this time to say, "If any man thirst, let him come unto Me, and drink. He that believeth on Me, as the Scripture hath said, out of his belly shall flow rivers of living water" (John 7:37-38).

Determined not to be hearers of the Word only but also doers, the people accepted the challenge to obedience even though it required considerable inconvenience. The people of Jerusalem gathered branches and erected booths on the roofs of their homes or in their courtyards. The priests and Levites built theirs in the courts of the temple and the people from the country constructed huts in the broad squares before the Water Gate and the Gate of Ephraim (v. 16). Such a wholehearted celebration of the Feast of Tabernacles had not been held for 1,000 years, since the time of Joshua (v. 17).

The account of this ancient celebration in Jerusalem concludes with the observations that the Word of God was read to the people every day of the feast, the people continued in their obedience to it, and there was among them an atmosphere of great rejoicing (vv. 17b-18).

But obedience is sometimes costly. A gunner named Pierre was standing by his gun, during a 19th century siege of Paris, when the commander came up and said, "Gunner, do you see the bridge over there and the little shanty in a thicket to the left?" "I see it, sir," said Pierre, turning pale. "It's an enemy nest; hit it with a shell!" the commander ordered. Pierre turned paler still but aimed his gun carefully and then fired it. "Well hit, my man, well hit!" exclaimed the general. But then he noticed the tears running down the gunner's cheeks. "What's the matter, man?" "Pardon me, General," said Pierre, "it was my house—everything I owned in this world."

Are we willing to obey God's commands regardless of the cost?

Trust and obey, for there's no other way
to be happy in Jesus, but to trust and obey.

9

The Nation that Prays
Together Stays Together

J. Edgar Hoover, longtime director of the F.B.I., observed, "The spectacle of a nation praying is more awe-inspiring than the explosion of an atomic bomb. The force of prayer is greater than any possible combination of man-made or man-controlled powers, because prayer is man's greatest means of tapping the infinite resources of God. Invoking by prayer the mercy and might of God is our most efficacious means of guaranteeing peace and security for the harrassed and helpless people of the earth."

And that is what we see in chapter 9—the spectacle of a nation at prayer. The previous chapter demonstrated the power of the Word of God. Now the emphasis is on prayer as an ingredient of national revival. Formerly, the mood was one of great rejoicing as the people celebrated the Feast of Tabernacles; that quickly changed to a time of mourning and confession of sin.

In a similarly crucial period in the history of our country, Benjamin Franklin urged that the Constitutional Convention in Philadelphia be convened daily with prayer. He declared:

> I have lived for a long time, and the longer I live the more convincing proof I see of this truth, that God governs in the affairs of men. If a sparrow cannot fall to the ground without His notice, is it probable that an empire can rise without His aid? We have been assured in the Sacred Writings that 'Except the Lord build the house, they labour in vain that

build it.' I firmly believe this, and I also believe that without His concurring aid we shall proceed in this political building no better than the builders of Babel.

The nation of Israel was in a time of rebuilding, politically and spiritually, and the day of national humiliation and prayer described in this chapter played an important part. First, we observe the preparation of the people (vv. 1-3), followed by the prayer of penitence (vv. 4-31) and finally a plea for pity (vv. 32-38).

The Preparation of the People (9:1-3)

The sacred seventh month was not yet over. On the first day (8:2) the men, women, and children had gathered for the reading of the Law. On the second day (8:13), the leaders had reassembled to hear more of the Word of God. The Feast of Tabernacles was then celebrated from the 15th to the 22nd day (8:14; see Lev. 23:34). On the 24th day (9:1) the people, still sensitive to their needs, voluntarily regathered to give themselves to spiritual exercises.

The Feast of Tabernacles was the time for joy and rejoicing, but this assembly was for repentance and confession of sin. The Jews fasted to show self-mortification, wore sackcloth as a sign of mourning, and put dirt on their heads as a symbol of their deep distress (9:1). In contrast to what Ezra found when he came to Jerusalem in 458 (see Ezra 9:1), the Jews separated from strangers, namely heathen, who were to have no part in this national act of humiliation and confession (9:2). One writer comments that at this time the remnant probably reached "the highest moral state they ever occupied from the Babylonian captivity to the coming of Messiah."

The order of activity on this important day is summarized in verse 3. For three hours the people stood as the Scriptures were read to them, intent on learning more of the mind and will of God. Then for the next three hours they confessed their sins and worshiped the Lord. Once again, we note that the Word of God produced results in the hearts of the listeners. And the sequence of events is significant too. The Word and prayer need to be held in balance but it is important to hear God speaking to us before we speak to Him. Observed Dr. H. A. Ironside, a former, longtime pastor of Moody Church:

One who gives himself preeminently to the Word, neglecting prayer, will become heady and doctrinal—likely to quarrel about 'points,' and be occupied with theoretical Christianity to the hurt of his soul and the irritation of his brethren. On the other hand, one who gives himself much to prayer while neglecting the Word is likely to become exceedingly introspective, mystical, and sometimes fanatical. But he who reads the Word of God reverently and humbly, seeking to know the will of God, and then gives himself to prayer, confessing and judging what the Scriptures have condemned in his ways, words, and thoughts, will have his soul drawn out in worship also, and thus grow both in grace and in knowledge, becoming a well-rounded follower of Christ. Apart from a knowledge of the Word, prayer will lack exceedingly in intelligence; for the objective must ever precede the subjective, but not be divorced therefrom" (*Notes on the Book of Nehemiah* [New York: Loizeaux Brothers, 1946], pp. 96-97).

The Prayer of Penitence (9: 4-31)

The people were now prepared to join in a public prayer of penitence. Standing on a platform, a select group of Levites led first in an invocation of praise (v. 5), similar to those in Psalm 41:13 and 106:48. It also reminds us of the words Jesus taught His disciples, "Our Father who art in heaven, hallowed be Thy name" (Matt. 6:9). In our prayers we should always be occupied first with the character of God.

The adoration of God continued and He was extolled as the unique Creator and Preserver of all (v. 6). Thus began the longest prayer recorded in the Bible. Many believe we have here the words of Ezra, especially since the Septuagint (the Greek translation of the Old Testament) inserts the phrase, "And Ezra said" at the beginning of verse 6. A comparison with his prayer in Ezra 9 does show remarkable similarity. It is also interesting to note that the first section (vv. 6-11) appears in the Jewish liturgy as a portion of their daily morning prayers.

From the adoration of God in His majesty and power, the prayer next reviews the history of God's covenant dealings with Israel. It oscillates between the goodness of God and the rebellion of Israel through history. The emphasis is that God is the God of history, communicating to a nation through the events of her past.

The call of Abraham (vv. 7-8). The retrospective section of the prayer begins with God's dealings with Abram. God chose him, brought him out of Ur, gave him the name Abraham ("father of a multitude"), and made a covenant with him. That Abrahamic Covenant was central to God's dealings with the nation. It promised personal blessing to Abraham, national blessing to Israel, and universal blessing through the Messiah to all who would believe (see Gen. 12:1-3; Matt. 1:1). The Covenant pledged the everlasting continuation of Abraham's seed and their permanent possession of the land ((Gen. 17:7-8).

While there can be no doubt regarding the ultimate fulfillment of God's purposes for the Jew, the blessings of that Covenant in any given generation were conditional on obedience. Abraham served as a challenging example for Nehemiah's generation because the patriarch was obedient when God revealed His will. If the remnant did the same, they too would experience God's blessing. Obedience is always the passport to blessing.

Deliverance from Egypt (vv. 9-11). In his prayer, Ezra moved on to summarize the major events of the Exodus, emphasizing what God did. The people's plight grew worse and worse but God intervened as their Redeemer. He saw their affliction in Egypt and heard their cry for deliverance. Then he brought the plagues against Pharaoh. As they escaped, He divided the Red Sea and drowned the Egyptians who pursued them.

In the midst of this summary Ezra said, "So didst Thou get Thee a name" (9:10b). This explains why God intervened on behalf of the Hebrews. "There was more at stake in Israel's history than her national welfare. God's holy name and honor were to be vindicated. Pharaoh's cruel treatment of the Hebrews was the first major threat to the fulfillment of God's covenant promise. It was Satan's challenge to God's power and truth. And so the Lord's dealing with Egypt's king was more than a contest between Aaron and the Egyptian magicians, more than a clash of will between Moses and Pharaoh. It was spiritual warfare—God's reply to Satan's challenge" (*Bible Knowledge,* Oct.—Dec. 1968, p. 91).

The people listened with keen interest to this portion of the prayer, for though they were no longer in exile they still considered themselves to be in "great distress" (v. 37b). God's past deliverances renewed their hopes for the present and future.

Provision in the wilderness (vv. 12-21). Ezra's prayer reminded the people that God not only saved His children from the enemy, but also from the natural terrors of the wilderness such as famine, death by thirst, loss of direction, and from themselves and their rebellious ways. God's kindness was seen in the pillar of cloud and fire providing shelter from the heat by day, warmth and protection from wild beasts by night, as well as guidance for moving in the right direction (v. 12). He also gave them "right judgments, and true laws, good statutes and commandments" at Mount Sinai so that they might be instructed how to live in the Promised Land under God's blessing (vv. 13-14). Further, He amply provided for their physical needs with "bread from heaven" and water "out of the rock" (v. 15).

Yet the ungrateful Israelites rebelled. Ezra described that past generation as disobedient, forgetful, stubborn, and rebellious (v. 17). He cited two incidents as proof: the appointment of a captain at Kadesh-barnea to return to Egypt (the proposal of Numbers 14:4 was apparently adopted) and the erection of the golden calf at Mount Sinai and the identification of that calf as the deliverer of Israel (vv. 17-18). In both cases, the sin of Israel was heinous because it involved the forsaking of the Lord, the One who had done nothing but good for them.

But God did not forsake His people. In connection with both incidents of rebellion Ezra added, "Thou didst not forsake them." Instead, in addition to the pillar of cloud and fire, the manna and water, God gave weak and sinful Israel His "good Spirit" to instruct them (v. 20). How great was the forbearance and love of God even in caring for those who forfeited the opportunity to enter the land by their disobedience. "Yea, forty years didst Thou sustain them in the wilderness, so that they lacked nothing; their clothes waxed not old, and their feet swelled not" (v. 21).

Could the returned remnant have failed to make the application to themselves? They too were prone to wander, and surely rejoiced to be reminded of God's mercy and forgiveness.

Nor should we miss the relevance of this revelation of God's mercy and grace. A professional man had been active in an eastern church but was falsely accused of wrongdoing. In clearing himself he made some hasty and inadvisable decisions. Discouraged, he

moved to California feeling God was through with him because of
his mistakes. Then he heard a godly pastor speak on Jonah 3:1,
"And the Word of the Lord came unto Jonah the second time."
The pastor emphasized that God gave Jonah a second chance, another opportunity to serve Him. In a letter to that pastor the man
described his previous discouragement and then said, "You will
never know what Jonah 3:1 means to me now." The history of
Israel as well as the history of God's dealings with us shows that
He is an expert at forgiveness—He is "ready to pardon, gracious
and merciful."

Conquest of Canaan (vv. 22-25). From the wilderness experiences, Ezra's prayer moved on to the conquest. The Israelites
first overthrew the Amorites in Trans-Jordan, an event often recalled in Hebrew history. In keeping His promise to Abraham,
God multiplied His people and brought them into Canaan. They
subdued and possessed the land and then delighted themselves in
all they found there—"houses full of all goods, wells digged, vineyards, and oliveyards, and fruit trees in abundance" (v. 25).

Clearly, Israel realized that the conquest was not their work
but God's. So did the Psalmist who wrote, "For they got not the
land in possession by their own sword, neither did their own arm
save them; but Thy right hand, and Thine arm, and the light of Thy
countenance, because Thou hadst a favor unto them" (Ps. 44:3).

In addition, Moses warned Israel to beware lest their prosperity
would become their downfall (see Deut. 8). Tragically, it happened just that way. Israel "became fat" and then forgot God
(v. 25, see Deut. 32:15). They delighted in God's gifts but they
forgot the Giver.

Unfortunately, this is a common human tendency. Let us be
warned by Israel's failure lest we prize the Lord's blessings more
than we love the Lord Himself. After reciting some of the great
blessings of being justified by faith, Paul concluded with the ringing
affirmation, "And not only this, but we also exult in God through
our Lord Jesus Christ" (Rom. 5:11, NASB).

Failure under judges and prophets (vv. 26-31). Ezra's confession
of the sins of his people became more pointed as he reviewed what
happened after Israel settled in the land. Instead of obeying God's
commands they ignored Him and concentrated on their luxuries.
One writer summarizes this section: "So madly persistent was the

backsliding habit of Israel, so grandly continuous was the patient long-suffering of God."

The cyclical pattern of the period of the Judges can be readily seen. The sin of the people (v. 26) brought their servitude to oppressors (v. 27a). This in turn caused them to cry for deliverance (v. 27b) and God heard and sent deliverers or judges (v. 27c). Shamefully, the cycle recurred—sin (v. 28a), servitude (v. 28b), supplication (v. 28c), and salvation (v. 28d).

Israel's unfaithfulness is explained by the final verse of the Book of Judges, "every man did that which was right in his own eyes" (Jud. 21:25). The people refused to follow God's objective standard, and instead chose a subjective standard, their own feelings and opinions. This explains the religious apostasy, the moral awfulness, and the political anarchy of the times. And it explains the prevalence of the same conditions in our own society. How much better if God's words to Joshua had been followed, then and now: "This book of the Law shall not depart out of thy mouth; but thou shalt meditate therein day and night, that thou mayest observe to do according to all that is written therein; for then thou shalt make thy way prosperous, and then thou shalt have good success" (Josh. 1:8).

The period of the Judges was followed by the monarchy with Saul, David, and Solomon reigning before the nation was divided. The northern and southern kingdoms (Israel and Judah) then existed side by side. But the story was the same—repeated and persistent failure to obey God's commands (v. 29). So God spoke to them through the prophets, but they would not listen (v. 30). Finally, the Lord gave them "into the hand of the people of the lands"—Israel to the Assyrians in 722 B.C. and Judah to the Babylonians in 586 B.C. Yet that was not the end for Israel because God was a "gracious and merciful God" (v. 31b). In His good will He restored the Jews to their land, enabling them to rebuild the temple and the city walls.

Though this review of Israel's history leaves us with a discouraging picture of man, it gives us a magnificent view of God. He is revealed as the:

God of creation (v. 6),
God of grace (vv. 7-8),
God who answers prayer (v. 9),

God of deliverance (vv. 10-12),
God of revelation (vv. 13-14),
God who supplies needs (v. 15),
God of mercy (vv. 17, 19, 27-28, 31).

Especially heartwarming is the truth emphasized in verse 31, that the Lord showed mercy to His people because it is His nature to be merciful.

Sometimes it is against our natures to be merciful. A mother once approached Napoleon seeking a pardon for her son. The emperor replied that it was a second offense and that justice demanded death. "But I don't ask for justice," explained his mother, "I plead for mercy." "But," declared the emperor, "he does not deserve mercy." "Sir," cried the mother, "it would not be mercy if he deserved it, and mercy is all I ask for." "Well then," said Napoleon, "I will have mercy." And her son was spared.

Christians are the recipients, not of justice—for that would mean certain condemnation—but of mercy. "Not by works of righteousness which we have done, but according to His mercy He saved us" (Titus 3:5).

The Plea for Pity (9: 32-38)

With the word "now" (v. 32), Ezra's prayer turned abruptly from remote history to the present. His intercession took the form of an appeal to God because of the plight of His people. The appeal was based on God's majesty ("the great, the mighty, the terrible God"); God's faithfulness ("who keepest covenant"); and God's compassion ("who keepest . . . mercy"). Ezra prayed that such a great God would not disregard the problems of His people, thinking them minor and of no significance.

But God is not, nor ever has been, indifferent to the needs of His children. Jesus assured His disciples that His Father was not unmindful of one sparrow falling to the ground, and added, "Fear ye not therefore, ye are of more value than many sparrows" (Matt. 10:31).

Ezra followed with a confession of sin (vv. 33-35), nationwide in scope and including various levels of society: the kings, princes, priests, and their forefathers (v. 34). In effect Ezra declared, "We deserved all we received! We brought it on ourselves by our wickedness."

The confession of Ezra reminds us of the prayer known as the General Confession in the standard edition of *The Book of Common Prayer*. In part it reads:

The Scriptures moveth us in sundry places to acknowledge and confess our manifold sins and wickedness. We should not dissemble nor cloke them . . . We have erred, and strayed from Thy ways like lost sheep. We have left undone those things which we ought to have done; and we have done those things which we ought not to have done; and there is no health in us. And forgive us our trespasses, as we forgive them that trespass against us.

Finally, Ezra lamented the present condition of the people. Even though they had been released from Babylonian bondage, they were still servants to the king of Persia (v. 36). As such they were heavily taxed (v. 37a) and subject to forced labor and compulsory military service (v. 37b). With a cry of anguish, "we are in great distress," Ezra begged for pity, resting the whole case with God.

But there is more. The solemn review of Israel's history brought the people to a new spiritual commitment to God. For the time, at least, Israel determined to learn from her past and obey God more perfectly in the future. Preparations were made to put their purpose in writing (v. 38).

Paul, reviewing Israel's history, wrote, "Now these things happened to them as an example, and they were written for our instruction, upon whom the ends of the ages have come" (1 Cor. 10:11, NASB). Paul affirmed that in the events of biblical history God speaks to us. What does He say? The answer is clear from this New Testament passage (1 Cor. 10:6-10)—there are five warnings that Israel's history gives us.

The first warning is that we should not lust: "to the intent we should not lust after evil things as they also lusted" (1 Cor. 10:6). This is probably a reference to Numbers 11. Israel had the manna, and that was God's gracious provision. But they were not satisfied with manna and wanted meat to eat. This was a craving after an evil thing. Not that the eating of meat was evil, but it was beyond what God had provided. And Paul warned that we should not crave that which God has not provided for us.

The second warning is that we should not commit idolatry: "neither be idolators as were some of them; as it is written, 'The people sat down to eat and drink and rose up to play' " (1 Cor. 10:7). Surely this is a reference to Exodus 32. Moses was up on the mountain receiving the Law of God. The people grew impatient. They thought he had disappeared forever. So they went to Aaron and asked him to make a god for them—so they could worship and find guidance for life. A golden calf became their god as they fell into idolatry—a practice that was stamped on the history of the nation.

Paul told the Corinthian church, "Neither be idolators." They too were tempted, for as we know from the background of this chapter they were invited to participate in idol festivals in the temples of Corinth. But Paul said, "Flee from idolatry" (1 Cor. 10:14). Believers today are warned in 1 John 5:21, "Little children, keep yourselves from idols." It is possible for us to put some things ahead of God. But the Bible solemnly warns, "Neither be idolators."

The third warning is to avoid immorality. "Neither let us commit fornication, as some of them committed, and fell in one day three and twenty thousand" (1 Cor. 10:8). This is a reference, no doubt, to Numbers 25. The Children of Israel were now the new generation, poised and ready to enter the Promised Land, to receive at long last this homeland, and then they fell into immorality. The men of Israel had intercourse with the women of Moab. There was even a man of Israel who dared bring a pagan woman right into the midst of the camp. God sent rapid and massive punishment in which 24,000 people died, 23,000 in one day.

Another warning is against unbelief: "Neither let us tempt Christ as some of them also tempted, and were destroyed of serpents" (1 Cor. 10:9). The word "tempted" here means to see how far they could go. They were testing God, to see how long they could complain and murmur against God and His leaders, Moses and Aaron. God said, "That's enough!" and He sent the serpents.

Complaining is also warned against: "Neither murmur ye, as some of them also murmured and were destroyed of the destroyer" (1 Cor. 10:10). Incredibly, after the destruction of Korah and his household, the Children of Israel complained bitterly against

God that He had so dealt with Korah. Judgment fell, destroying 14,700 Israelites.

These are the warnings from Israel's history. The man who is only concerned with the present and not the past is extremely shortsighted, because history contains valuable lessons for us. Chiefly, it demonstrates that God is the Lord of history who intervenes in national and personal life.

The Spanish Armada was anchored off the coast of England. The history of the British Empire, as well as our own, would have been changed had not a storm descended destroying the Spanish fleet.

Columbus would have landed on the shores of Virginia or the Carolinas, had not a flight of pigeons changed his direction to the West Indies. That the Spanish flag was not placed on the soil of this country altered the course of American history.

God not only moves in the affairs of nations; He intervenes in the lives of people. Two federal prisoners visited our church recently to thank us for providing funds to send them to Washington, D.C. to a seminar sponsored by Charles Colson. One was a banker who clashed with the law and was sentenced to five years in prison. The class listened intently as he told the story of his life. Raised in south Texas, his family only knew a "bellhop God" ("We only called Him when we needed Him"). He achieved success in athletics in high school and university and later served as a coach for several years.

Then a friend introduced him to banking. Driving hard to get to the top, he became president of the bank at age 30. Then came the dark day when, after two years of fighting the charges of violating banking laws, he was pronounced guilty and sentenced to prison. But in that prison he found Jesus Christ, and he said, "I let loose of everything and turned my life over to God." He is now teaching Bible classes in the prison and hopes for an early release in order to further train to serve the Lord.

Have *you* traced the course of God's dealings in your life recently? Have you considered making a "sure covenant," as the Jews of old, to obey God more perfectly and to serve Him more faithfully?

10
Put It in Writing

NATION PLEDGES ALLEGIANCE TO TORAH; FIRST KNESSET OPENS IN JERUSALEM

Intermarriage Banned; Work on Sabbath Outlawed; Temple Offerings Reinstituted

The nation's leaders, 120 in number, today solemnly placed their signatures on a document formulated by Ezra the Scribe, which obliges the people of Judah to regulate their lives according to the Torah—the Law of Moses.

The main points of the Covenant are the following: (1) prohibition of mixed marriages; (2) observance of the Sabbath—binding on all citizens of Judah, including Gentiles; (3) reinstitution of the Sabbatical Year, affecting lands and monetary debts; (4) reinstitution of temple tithes and offerings.

The historic signing ceremony brought to an end a series of great events that commenced on the first day of the month, when Ezra began reading the Torah, word for word, to the assembled masses.

The reading of the Torah was followed by the Succoth Festival (15-22 Tishri), which this year was celebrated with unusual fervor. Jerusalem was filled to overflowing with people who had come here to be present at the reading of the Torah and the signing of the Covenant.

Yesterday, on the 25th day of Tishri of the year 3317 of the Creation (142 years after the destruction of the First Temple, and 72 years after the dedication of the Second Temple), Ezra and Nehemiah appointed the Great Assembly (*Knesset Gedolah*) to represent the people in matters of national legislation.

Today the 120 members of the Assembly, acting on behalf of the people of Judah signed the Covenant which, in essence, is a pledge of allegiance to the Law of Moses.

The Covenant goes into effect as of now. (*Chronicles; News of the Past*. Jerusalem: The Reuboni Foundation.)

If there had been a newspaper called *The Jerusalem Chronicle* in the time of Nehemiah, the report of the signing of the covenant might have been similar to this account. The covenant was the climax in the spiritual revival that occurred in this memorable seventh month of the Jewish sacred year. As with any true revival, it possessed three essential ingredients: (1) it was based on the Word of God, not on mere emotion (chap. 8); (2) it involved confession of sin to God (chap. 9); and (3) it produced obedience to the Scriptures in the form of practical application of what they had heard (chap. 10).

G. Campbell Morgan, the late British commentator, summarized these three crucial chapters, "In the light of the Law, as it was expounded on the day of *convocation*, and in the power of the approach to God on the day of *humiliation*, the people entered into covenant on the day of *dedication*" (*An Exposition of the Whole Bible* [New Jersey: Fleming H. Revell Co., 1959], p. 195).

Chapter 10 of Nehemiah describes a spiritual commitment, with the people taking specific and concrete steps to do the will of God. They did not hesitate to put their agreement with God in writing, thus declaring their solemn intentions in a public manner and fixing them vividly in their own minds. The company of the committed is listed first, and then the nature of their commitment follows.

The Signers of the Covenant (10:1-27)

The drawing up of the covenant about to be signed is explained in the last verse of the previous chapter. Ezra concluded his magnif-

icent and moving prayer of penitence by affirming that in spite
of all the troubles that had overtaken Israel, they retained their
faith in God and prepared this "sure covenant" as a declaration
of their purpose to follow Him more wholeheartedly than in the
past.

Nehemiah the Tirshatha (governor), who had been in the background during this time of spiritual revival, set a proper example
for others by being the first to sign (v. 1). He was followed by
Zidkyah (Zikdijah), thought to have been his secretary. Indivi-
dually, these men and the rest set their personal seal to the
document or as some suggest, they attached their signature or
mark on the seal according to the ancient practice of making a
thumbnail imprint in the clay of cuneiform business tablets. Nehemiah's leadership here (did he assist in the writing of the covenant?) affirms the fact that as the highest civil authority under
the king, he was concerned for far more than civil order and
physical security. The spiritual defenses of the people must be
repaired as well.

Next to sign were 21 priests who were heads of priestly households (vv. 2-8). The fact that Ezra's name does not appear indicates that he apparently was not the head of a household.

The names of 17 heads of Levitical households appear next
(vv. 9-13). These teachers of the Law were anxious to sign the
covenant, affirming obedience to its requirements.

The final group to sign consisted of 44 heads of leading lay
families (vv. 14-27). These leaders too accepted the responsibility
of being examples before the other citizens of Jerusalem.

A man who advertised for a gardener received a letter from a
friend recommending someone who possessed great abilities in
this area. Listed in minute detail were the gardener's experience
and what he was capable of doing in the planting and cultivation
of various types of gardens. The man who received the letter
exclaimed with delight, "This is the man I've been looking for;
he can do the very things I want done." When he turned the
letter over there were three words on that side—"But he won't!"

While there were probably some who refused to sign the "sure
covenant" saying in effect, "We won't obey the Law," the long
list constitutes an honor roll of leaders and heads of households
committed to obedience. They joined Joshua, who had stated

years before, "As for me and my house, we will serve the Lord"
(Josh. 24:15b).

The Features of the Covenant (10:28-39)

Together with those listed specifically by name, the "rest of the
people" now came forward to declare their spiritual commitment.
Though these did not sign the document, they, along with their
leaders, bound themselves by a solemn oath to keep the conditions
of the covenant (v. 29a).

Essentially, the covenant had four provisions, one general and
three specific. The people promised to live in subjection to the
Word of God, to avoid intermarriage with the heathen, to keep the
Sabbath law, and to support the temple.

Subjection to the Word of God (v. 29b). The people pledged
themselves to "observe and do all the commandments of the
LORD our Lord, and His judgments and His statutes." That was
a sizable order in view of their past record of fickleness and disobedience of Gods Laws. But in view of their past history of
chastisement under God's hand it was a necessary commitment.
They could not expect God to bless them apart from this decision
to live under the authority of the Scriptures. Moses had warned
their fathers of this centuries before (see Deut. 28). Had this
generation at last learned that God meant what He said?

Separation from mixed marriages (v. 30). Admittedly, it is
easier to make general promises than specific ones, but the covenant now made that kind of exacting transition. It focused next
on what was probably the burning issue of the day—intermarriage
with the peoples of the land. Because it was one of the most
persistent problems that plagued the post exilic community, Ezra
had had to deal with it (see Ezra 9—10), and Nehemiah too
would later face it (chapter 13). The practice had been clearly
forbidden in the Scriptures (see Ex. 34:12-16; Deut. 7:3; Josh.
23:12; Jud. 3:6). Only wilful disobedience could account for the
periodic violation of this prohibition that was so essential to the
preservation of godly families and, ultimately, the national identity
of Israel as a people under God.

Sabbath observance (v. 31). The fourth commandment charged
Israel to keep the seventh day sacred as a memorial to God's rest
on the seventh day of creation week (Ex. 20:8-11), and later as

a memorial of the nation's redemption out of Egypt (Deut. 5:15). It was the observance of the Sabbath that reminded the Jews of their unique calling as a special people of Jehovah and set them apart from the heathen. But along with other commandments of the Law, the keeping of this one had apparently been violated, and the covenant was intended to rectify that problem. Three particulars regarding the Sabbath Law are mentioned as a part of the covenant.

First, in view of the apparent fact that foreigners had brought their wares into Jerusalem on the Sabbath, influencing the Jews to violate the day by buying and selling, they pledged to cease this practice. Further, they promised to "leave the seventh year," that is, they vowed to leave their fields uncultivated during the sabbatical year (see Lev. 25:1-7). This year was called a "Sabbath unto the Lord" and was designed to remind Israel that God was the owner and they the tenants of the land; "For the earth is the Lord's and the fullness thereof" (Ps. 24:1). Finally, they affirmed that they would forgo the collection of debts during the sabbatical years (see Deut. 15:1-4). This was a severe test of faith for the Jews because these provisions, and those yet to come, would cost them dearly. They met the challenge, however, and placed themselves under this covenant regardless of the cost.

Support of the temple (vv. 32-39). It is significant to note that by signing this covenant the people surrendered their pocketbooks. Apparently, the revival had struck deep.

A Christian businessman was being audited by the Internal Revenue Service. The agent scrutinized the list of contributions and then saw another list of donations. "What are these?" he inquired. "Oh, those are contributions that don't qualify for a deduction," was the reply. The agent thought for a moment, closed his books and left. Here was a man who knew what stewardship meant.

The Jews demonstrated by four particulars that they were good stewards.

1. They promised to pay a temple tax (vv. 32-33). The funds required for the temple services had been provided by the Persian court but the Jews now recognized their own responsibility in this matter. Perhaps the Scripture reading had included the passage from Exodus stating that an assessment of one-half shekel

was imposed on all males 20 years old and above for the support of the tabernacle (Ex. 30:11-16). While the Jews in Nehemiah's time resolved to pay one-third shekel, it should be recognized that this is not a discrepancy nor a deviation from the standard of the Torah. Rather, the Persian one-third skekel was equivalent in weight to the Hebrew one-half skekel. The objects for which the tax was to be spent are listed in verse 33.

2. They vowed to bring a wood offering (v. 34). With reference to the brazen alter, the Lord said to Moses: "And the fire upon the altar shall be burning in it; it shall not be put out; and the priest shall burn wood on it every morning and lay the burnt offering in order upon it; and he shall burn thereon the fat of the peace offerings. The fire shall ever be burning upon the altar; it shall never go out" (Lev. 6:12-13).

The supply of wood for the large number of sacrifices was no small concern. The Jews did not occupy a large territory, and the forests in the vicinity of Jerusalem were no doubt severely damaged during the Babylonian siege. Josephus states that a day was observed as "the festival of wood-bringing, at which the custom was for every one to bring wood for the altar, that there might never be a want of fuel for the fire which was unquenched and always burning" (*Jewish War* II. 17.6). According to the Mishnah (rabbinic interpretation of Scripture), there were nine such days in a year when the wood supply was replenished. A decision was to be made by casting lots to determine the order in which the households were to supply the wood.

3. They pledged offerings of firstfruits to be brought to the temple (vv. 35-36). The firstfruits of the ground were given to Jehovah as an acknowledgment of Him as Landlord, much like the first mowings of a field that were paid to the king (Amos 7:1). The fact that the firstfruits of all trees were given to God was a demonstration of their deep earnestness, since the Law specified only seven trees from which firstfruits were to be dedicated. The firstborn sons belonged to the Lord too, but were redeemed by the payment of five shekels and the money was given to the priests (Ex. 13:13; Num. 18:15). The firstborn of animals were brought to the temple where oxen, sheep, and goats were sacrificed and other unclean animals redeemed (see Num. 18:15, 17-19).

4. They committed themselves to bring offerings for the priests

and Levites (vv. 37-39). The offerings described above were for sacrificial purposes whereas these were for the support and use of the priests and Levites. It was further provided that the Levites who received the tithes in the scattered rural villages were in turn to bring a tenth to the temple for the priests, porters, and singers who ministered there (see Num. 18:26-29).

In summary of the final part of the "sure covenant," the Jews solemnly affirmed, "We will not forsake the house of our God" (v. 39b). Their history taught them that to neglect the temple meant to neglect the worship of Jehovah which centered there. They seemed determined for the time at least, to avoid the consequences of that mistake again and made this total commitment of support for the Lord's house.

Personal stewardship continues to be a reliable index of commitment to the Lord and His work. The believer today is not under the law of the tithe but that does not leave us without instruction in the matter of our giving. In 1 Corinthians 16, Paul gave the following directions to the believers at Corinth: (1) he stated the need (16:1); (2) he asked them to give (16:1b); (3) he instructed each one to participate (16:2a); (4) he advised them to give proportionately to their income or wealth without specifying a percentage (16:2b); (5) and he counseled the appointment of certain trustworthy men to handle the funds (16:3-4).

Our giving to the Lord's work should be regular and not spasmodic. During the Civil War, just after the second battle of Bull Run, a letter arrived from Stonewall Jackson at the post office in his home town, addressed to his pastor. The telegraph lines were all down and the people had been waiting anxiously for news. They recognized General Jackson's handwriting and pressed the pastor to open the letter. The seal was broken disclosing the following news: "Dear Pastor, I remember that this is the day of the collection for foreign missions. Please find enclosed my check. T. J. Jackson." Even in the midst of battle Stonewall Jackson did not neglect the work of the Lord.

During my first year of teaching at a small college the dean often sent memos to the faculty with the following instruction printed across the top: "DON'T SAY IT; WRITE IT!" In this chapter, the Jews did exactly that. To demonstrate their spiritual commitment, they put it in writing and many signed their names. They meant business with God.

A faculty colleague at our seminary advises his students and other serious Christians to make an appointment with God just as we do to see other people. He urges, "If your first appointment on the daily calendar is for 8:30 A.M. then write 'Appointment with God' at 8:00 A.M. Postponements are allowed but not cancellations!"

"This practice has transformed my life," declares the professor. It will yours too—but put it in writing.

11
Where Should We Live?

A young Christian worker and his wife were burdened to start a Bible-teaching church in New England and shared their vision with friends in Texas, a dental technician and wife, asking them to consider joining with them in the project. But giving up a prosperous business and moving to a cold and remote part of the country was too much at first for the couple to contemplate, especially when they had not even seen snow. Then it happened. Without warning or provocation, the business completely dried up and a brief exploratory trip to Maine brought four or five immediate job offers. God was obviously directing them to relocate and they responded obediently. They joined the pastor and his wife in establishing a new testimony for Christ in a needy area.

The relocation of some of the Jewish population to live in Jerusalem was next on Nehemiah's agenda. Previously, it was noted that "the city was large and great; but the people were few therein, and the houses were not builded" (Neh. 7:4). Nehemiah purposed to increase the population to make the city less vulnerable to attack, to provide adequate personnel for the temple and its services, and to make Jerusalem a strong and beautiful capital—a symbol of their national unity.

The events of the sacred season, the seventh month, interrupted the plans (see chap. 8—10), but they resumed again, and were carried through with the precision and dispatch that characterized Nehemiah's earlier leadership activities.

Jerusalem was not the most popular place to live; the masses of people evidently preferred to reside elsewhere. In the capital, the cost of living was no doubt higher, there was a housing shortage, jobs were not plentiful, and personal safety could not be guaranteed. Nehemiah, as governor, coud have arbitrarily ordered certain families to sell their homes and land and move to the city, but he did not. The whole movement seems to have been a volunteer one, though it is difficult not to imagine Nehemiah behind the scenes using gentle, persuasive reasoning.

We are told that the rulers dwelt at Jerusalem (11:1). It has been suggested that these leaders volunteered to move there as a result of the meeting mentioned earlier (see 7:5). But that did not increase the population sufficiently to guarantee the defense of Jerusalem and to restore its status as the religious and civic capital of the land.

A second step provided for casting lots so that one in ten (probably family units) would leave the countryside and move to the "holy city" (11:1). Apparently, the goal was to have a capital city containing one tenth of the community population. By participating in casting lots, the people voluntarily sought the will of God in the matter of the proposed move, remembering no doubt the words of Proverbs 16:33: "The lot is cast into the lap; but the whole disposing thereof is of the Lord."

In addition, it seems that others volunteered out of patriotic motives to move to Jerusalem and for that they received grateful thanks from their brethren (11:2). Nehemiah himself, according to Josephus, went out of his way to make provision for the new inhabitants even to the extent of building them homes.

While we should not minimize the personal difficulties that must have been involved in the relocation of so many families, it is instructive to remember that their chief concern was to live where God wanted them to. One writer has aptly commented, "The place for anyone to live is the place of God's appointment. We must be willing to live where He wants us, whether it is in Secaucus, New Jersey, or Walla Walla, Washington, or Timbuktu, Africa." Are we willing to put even that in the hands of our God?

Turning from the statement of general methodology for the urban renewal of Jerusalem, Nehemiah moved on toward the culmination of his goals. He recorded first the registers of Jewish citizens both in and out of Jerusalem (11:3—12:26); then he related what happened at the dedication of the completed walls of Jerusalem (12:27-43); and finally he described the organization of the temple support (12:44-47).

Register of Jewish Citizens (11: 3—12: 26)

Is the register of Jewish citizens another dry rehearsal of names to be passed by quickly for something more exciting? Hardly. This is a list of individuals who were entered on God's honor roll because of their sensitivity to God's will, because they were eager to be in the place of God's appointment performing the service He had called them to do.

Residents of Jerusalem (11:3-24). Included in this choice company were the rulers (vv. 3-9), priests (vv. 10-14), Levites (vv. 15-18), porters (gatekeepers) and Nethinims (temple servants) (vv. 19-21), and certain officials appointed by the king of Persia (vv. 22-24).

Once again, the superb administrative abilities of Nehemiah were demonstrated. It was not enough to have a division of responsibility for the rebuilding of the walls. At best, though that task was difficult, it was soon finished. The greater problem was to maintain a well-ordered city, no small task as the officials of any modern metropolis would testify. Skillfully, Nehemiah arranged for the systematic division and assignment of duties. Some were needed to do the "work of the house" (v. 12), namely to attend to the sacrifices. Others were counted on for the defense of the city (v. 14). One was appointed to lead the choir (v. 17), and others had the responsibility of providing materials for repairing the temple (v. 16). Another group guarded the gates (v. 19) while some provided oversight of the ministry of the temple (v. 22). Special mention is made of a Judean who served as an official representative of Jewish interests at the Persian Court (v. 24).

Thus we have a fresh illustration of how things may be done "decently and in order" in the Lord's work. It is not a question of depending on the leaders to do it all, for they cannot possibly cover all the bases. Peter crisply summarized the matter, "As every man hath received the gift, even so minister the same one to another, as good stewards of the manifold grace of God" (1 Peter 4:10).

Residents outside Jerusalem (11:25-36). With the Jerusalem residents listed, the villages settled by the Jews outside the capital were then named. The settlements were scattered in the south, (the Negeb); in the hill country (the Shephelah); in the mountains near Jerusalem on the north and west; and in the coastal plain on the west. In these areas lived those of the tribes of Judah (vv. 25-30) and Benjamin (vv. 31-36).

There were no second-class citizens. It was essential that the majority of the population live outside Jerusalem in rural towns and villages, farming the land and raising animals for food and sacrifice. Not all could live in the city made holy by the temple and the presence of the Lord. Some, in the will of God, had to live elsewhere and they too were honored servants of God.

Priests and Levites of Zerubbabel's return (12:1-9). Why should the heads and families of priests and Levites who came to Jerusalem with Zerubbabel nearly 100 years previously, in 536 B.C., be inserted here? Matthew Henry suggested that this register was "to keep in remembrance those good men, that posterity might know to whom they were beholden, under God, for the happy revival and re-establishment of their religion among them . . . Perhaps it is intended to stir up their posterity, who succeeded them in the priest's office and inherited their dignities and preferments, to imitate their courage and fidelity."

Nehemiah had a sense of history and he wished to preserve it in writing for the benefit of the present and future generations. The New Testament writers had the same burden and remind us often of the importance of remembering those who walked and labored by faith before us. Hebrews 11, for example, leads us on a magnificent and moving journey through the Old Testament reminding us how Abel, Enoch, Noah, Abraham, Isaac, Jacob, Joseph, Moses, and many others set an example of walking faith in their respective generations. The writer of that epistle also urges us not to forget more recent leaders. "Remember those who led you, who spoke the Word of God to you; and considering the outcome of their way of life, imitate their faith" (Heb. 13:7, NASB).

Between the many biblical heroes of faith and our more recent spiritual leaders are many stalwarts of church history, unfortunately only scarcely known by the average Christian. Who could measure the spiritual benefits that would come from more than a passing acquaintance with Athanasius, Chrysostom, Augustine of Hippo, Anselm of Canterbury, Martin Luther, John Knox, John Calvin, George Whitefield, Jonathan Edwards, John and Charles Wesley, William Carey, Charles Haddon Spurgeon, and others?

Postexilic high priests (12:10-11). After listing priests and Levites of Zerubbabel's time, Nehemiah included high priests who held that office after the exile. The roster of high priests in 1 Chronicles 6 concludes with Jehozadak who was taken into captivity. In order to bring matters up-to-date, the roll began with Joshua, the first high priest after the captivity (see Ezra 2:2; Hag. 1:1; Zech. 3:1) and concluded with Jaddua, a contemporary with Nehemiah.

Many assume that this Jaddua was the high priest when Alexander the Great passed through Palestine on his way to Egypt. Josephus tells of a supposed meeting in Jerusalem between Alexander and the high priest Jaddua (*Ant.*, X1. 8.5). But Alexander's conquests came about 100 years after Nehemiah's day. Are we to assume that Jaddua was a mere infant when Nehemiah recorded the high priests and that he lived over 100 years? Should we accept the suggestion of some that Jaddua was not yet born and that this is therefore a later addition of some future editor? If we assume Josephus to be correct in naming Jaddua as high priest in Alexander's time—and it should be remembered that Josephus is not always trustworthy—then why could there not be a son of the same name as the high priest contemporary with Nehemiah? At any rate, it can be affirmed that there is no valid reason for redating the book to a later time or for asserting that Nehemiah could not have written everything in this chapter as well as in the entire book.

Priests and Levites after Zerubbabel and Jeshua (12:12-26). As previously discussed, we have a record of priests and Levites in the time of Zerubbabel the prince and Jeshua the high priest in 12:1-9. Nehemiah completed the register by including priests and Levites under succeeding high priests. Heads of priestly houses are given in verses 12-21, and heads of Levitical families in verses 22-26.

Many people do not understand the meaning or importance of lists of names. A small boy asked his pastor about a plaque in the lobby of his church. The pastor replied that it contained the names of all the people who had died in the service. "Which one," asked the boy, "the 11 o'clock or the 7:30?"

Names always have significance, and while many of them in these registers may not be meaningful to us, they were important in their time not only to their generation but especially to God. Malachi the prophet, a contemporary of Nehemiah, made mention of those who in the midst of spiritual declension (see Neh. 13) were faithful: "Then they that feared the Lord spoke often one to another; and the Lord hearkened, and heard it, and a book of remembrance was written before Him for them that feared the Lord, and that thought upon His name" (Mal. 3:16).

Would we qualify for listing in that "book of remembrance"?

Dedication of Jerusalem's Walls (12: 27-43)

The solemn but glad day of dedication arrived at last. It was a time of exhilaration emotionally, but more than that, it was an experience that bound the people together in a deeper unity and caused them to reflect on their unique blessing as the people of God.

Since no date is given for the dedication, various intervals after the completion of the walls have been proposed. Some even suggest it took place 12 years later and was the occasion for Nehemiah's return from Persia for his second term as governor. But among the ancient Hebrews, dedication rites were considered the final act of building (see Deut. 20:5) and it is only natural to assume the ceremony took place soon after the walls were rebuilt. Since this was accomplished in the sixth month (6:15) and the solemn religious assemblies were held in the seventh month (7:73b), it is probable that these religious convocations concluded with the ceremony of dedication.

The assembling of Levites and musicians (vv. 27-29). The organizational skills of Nehemiah can be seen again, for almost certainly he was the one who planned the massive and moving ceremony of consecration. Word was sent throughout the countryside concerning this momentous occasion, and people began to gather in Jerusalem from scattered villages and farms. Nehemiah called in particular for more Levites to assist in the religious rites and also for the "sons of the singers," perhaps a guild of choristers, because music was to have a prominent part in the dedication. And they came with their musical instruments, cymbals, psalteries, and harps.

The rites of purification (v. 30). Before the dedication there had to be a ritual purification. First the priests and Levites purified themselves, probably by fasting, washing their clothes, and bringing sacrifices (see Num. 8:21). Then the process extended to the people, gates, and walls of the city. The ritual for the people no doubt included washing themselves and their clothes (see Num. 19:12, 19). The gates and walls were probably sprinkled with blood (see the purification of the temple in the reign of Hezekiah, 2 Chron. 29:20-24).

All of this was necessary because of man's defilement. How many of us are sensitive to the need for spiritual cleansing before participating in the ministry of the Word, whether that might involve singing in the church choir, teaching a Sunday School class, or preaching from the pulpit?

The ritual procession (vv. 31-39). Nehemiah next divided the people and their leaders into two companies. The staging area for the great procession was apparently near the Valley Gate at the southwest corner of the city. With Ezra a part of one group and Nehemiah attached to the other, the groups each had, in order, a choir (vv. 31, 38a), a civic official leading half of the lay leaders (vv. 32, 38, 40), seven priests (vv. 33-34, 41), and eight Levites (vv. 35-36a, 42).

Mounting the walls, one company (v. 31b) went counterclockwise, as Nehemiah had gone when he first came to Jerusalem (cf. 2:13-15). The other company (v. 38) went clockwise, covering, as did the other group, about half the circumference of the wall. Both groups met in the court of the temple where the dedication service would take place.

It is probable that the walk around the walls was accompanied by instrumental music and that the people sang songs of thanksgiving as they went. No doubt they were also reminded of their own labors in helping repair the walls and gates and of God's faithfulness in protecting them from the enemies who tried to harass the builders and hinder the work.

Observes one writer, "How similar this situation may be in our lives today! For those who have had an active part in building the church of Christ, whether in a physical or spiritual way, or both, how much more meaningful that church becomes to us! When we have put a part of ourselves into it—physically, emotionally, and spiritually—we have a real concern for the church and the cause of Christ" (Paul A. Stewart, *Nehemiah, the Involved Layman*, p. 129).

The dedication ceremony (vv. 40-43). Standing at last in the temple courts, the service began with singing led by the choir and joined by all the people.

The whole ceremony is punctuated with outbursts of praise and song. The instruments of music were used to give notes of inspiration and confidence. Imagine the large numbers of people engaged in singing like a festival of song. The Welsh people who lived in London a few years ago gathered in the Royal Albert Hall just to sing. With an organ and a song leader five thousand people sang the favorite hymns to the familiar tunes so characteristic of Wales. This was not a trained choir but only people gathered to sing! The recording of that festival is one that thrills the heart. Thus Israel gathered that day in Jerusalem to sing God's praises" (Ralph G. Turnbull, *The Book of Nehemiah*, Grand Rapids: Baker Book House, 1968, pp. 96-97).

And what did the people sing? Without question appropriate psalms were used, such as the beautiful Psalm 122 (NASB).

I was glad when they said to me,
"Let us go to the house of the Lord."
Our feet are standing
Within your gates, O Jerusalem,
Jerusalem, that is built
As a city that is compact together;
To which the tribes go up, even the tribes of the Lord—
An ordinance for Israel—
To give thanks to the name of the Lord.
For there thrones were set for judgment,

The thrones of the house of David.
Pray for the peace of Jerusalem:
"May they prosper who love you.
May peace be within your walls,
And prosperity within your palaces."
For the sake of my brothers and my friends,
I will now say, "May peace be within you."
For the sake of the house of the Lord our God
I will seek your good.

Music was an important part of their worship on this day of celebration and it should be a vital part of our worship, both private and corporate. When David brought the Ark of the Covenant into Jerusalem he sang,

Give thanks unto the Lord, call upon His name;
Make known His deeds among the peoples.
Sing to Him, sing praises to Him;
Speak of all His wonders.
Glory in His holy name;
Let the heart of those who seek the Lord be glad.
Seek the Lord and His strength;
Seek His face continually (1 Chron. 16:8-11, NASB).

Another important part of the dedication ceremony was the offering of sacrifices. These were probably not burnt offerings but peace offerings, in connection with which the people shared in a communion meal. It was an occasion for great rejoicing and everyone, including wives and children, took part. So great is the stress on joy that Nehemiah referred to it five times (in verb and noun form) in this one verse (43). Were there some who thought such an emotional display improper? In our own sophisticated age, many would be afraid of such outward expression in worship, but emotion that springs from a heart that is occupied with the Lord and His works surely pleases Him.

Organization of Temple Support (12: 44-47)

The walls of Jerusalem had been dedicated in a glorious service of consecration, and the people took steps to make certain that those

who served at the temple—the priests, Levites, singers, and porters—were cared for. Men were appointed as the regular receivers
and custodians of the firstfruits and tithes.

Appreciation of their faithful service motivated the people to
contribute to the support of the temple workers (vv. 44-45). In
matters of religious activity, including temple support, Nehemiah's
time is compared with what prevailed earlier under Zerubbabel
(v. 47).

Thus, the chapter closes on a spiritual mountaintop—the people
were purified, the walls dedicated, and a new enthusiasm and zeal
for the support of the Lord's work was manifested. What an ideal
place to conclude the story. But the end was not yet. One writer
observed,

> If the chronicler had laid down his pen at this point . . . his
> work might have presented a much more artistic appearance
> than it now wears. And yet it would have been artificial, and
> therefore false to the highest art of history. In adding a
> further extract from Nehemiah's memoirs that discloses a
> revival of the old troubles, and so shows that the evils against
> which the reformers contended had not been stamped out,
> the writer mars the literary effect of his record of their tri-
> umph; but, at the same time, he satisfies us that he is in con-
> tact with real life, its imperfections and its disappointments"
> (Walter F. Adeney, *Ezra, Nehemiah & Esther*, p. 339).

Though we are not prepared for what follows in the next and
final chapter, we nonetheless are forced to acknowledge that it is
all too true to life. There is no such thing as a final victory for the
Christian this side of heaven. Alertness is always necessary lest
our enemies overtake us and we fall from our own steadfastness
or stability. We are challenged by Peter to keep on growing "in
grace and in the knowledge of our Lord and Saviour Jesus Christ"
(2 Peter 3:18). And that is not an option but an imperative!

12

Challenge to a Permissive Society

It doesn't take a big person to be used of God . . .
But it takes all there is of him!
You don't need a five-foot pipeline to irrigate a garden . . .
You can do it with a quarter-inch hose . . .
Assuming an adequate source—a connection between it and
    the hose—and an uncluttered channel.
The only ability God requires is availability!
Because the resources are His—and they are unlimited!
In His providence He pours those resources through human
    channels who are willing to be used.
(Richard C. Halverson, "Perspective," January 18, 1978)

Nehemiah was just such a man—available and willing to be used of God. And the final chapter of the book bearing his name demonstrates how he was used to deliver his nation from a crisis more desperate than the one stemming from the collapsed walls. As we will see, Nehemiah returned to the Persian court after his governorship of 12 years. In his absence, the old evils returned as the people were gripped by permissiveness, "a condition of society which permits the open practice without shame, rebuke, or chastisement of what was once regarded as wrong." E. M. Blaiklock illustrates this definition with the account of a young Englishman who was in Germany when the Nazis degraded Jews publicly. He was at first sick at the sight and quickly turned away. The next time he stopped and looked for a full minute. Then he found himself standing with the jeering crowd, the sight seeming less revolting. Thus the young Englishman became permissive. Such permissiveness is "the beginning of the end, unless, intelligent enough, endowed sufficiently with courageous leadership, frightened enough, or swept by a revival of faith, a people rallies and returns to strength. Unless that happens, 'as surely as water will wet us, as surely as fire will burn,' that people dies." ("The Permissive Society," *The Alliance Witness,* October 5, 1977, p. 4).

Nehemiah provided that necessary intelligent and courageous leadership and valiantly cleansed the nation of serious abuses. It is clear that he firmly believed and applied the words of Solomon, "Righteousness exalteth a nation but sin is a reproach to any people" (Prov. 14:34).

Banishment of Foreigners (13:1-3)

The melancholy relapse of the people of Judah was characterized by failure in the area of their relationship with their heathen neighbors. It was a perennial problem, but when did that particular breakdown occur? The expression of verse 1, "on that day," would seem at first to relate it to the day of dedication of the previous chapter. But then the Levites were being given their portion (12:47), whereas on the "day" of this chapter they were not (13:10). We conclude that there is a gap of time between chapters 12 and 13 and that the chronological order of the events was as follows: (1) Nehemiah's leave of absence from the Persian court came to an end after 12 years and he returned to his post with Artaxerxes (see 2:6; 5:14; 13:6). (2) During the governor's absence from Judah, abuses quickly developed and spread widely. The abuses included a breakdown in separation described in the opening verses, as well as the other sad defections.

It is highly likely that Nehemiah once again heard disturbing reports about the state of affairs in Jerusalem as he served King Artaxerxes, and moved with the same compulsions as before, sought and received a second leave of absence (v. 6).

Since it does not appear that Nehemiah was on the scene when the first abuse was dealt with, we can suppose that this reform was accomplished while he was traveling toward Jerusalem, praying for God to intervene.

And intervene God did by raising up another man of God, Malachi the prophet. It is true that the prophet is not referred to by name, yet Bible scholars generally agree that Malachi stood with Nehemiah as Haggai and Zechariah stood with Zerubbabel and Joshua nearly a century earlier. The sins Malachi enumerated are identical to those Nehemiah encountered: an absence of godliness, especially among the priests (Mal. 1:6-8); the prevalence of foreign marriages (Mal. 2:10-12); and failure to pay tithes for temple support (Mal. 3:7-10).

On one of the days set aside for the public reading of the Law (v. 1, see Neh. 8) attention was called, probably by Malachi as well as others, to Deuteronomy 23:3-5, a portion of the "Book of Moses" which excluded Moabites and Ammonites from the congregation of Israel for the reasons cited (v. 2). It is interesting to observe this evidence both for the Mosaic authorship of Deuteronomy and for the fact that the first five books of the Old Testament were considered a unit and called "the Book of Moses."

The response of the leaders of the community to the Word of God was commendable (v. 3). They banished from Israel those who had intermarried with the Moabites and Ammonites and who were here called the "mixed multitude" or more literally, the "alien mixture." But why had this breach of the Law happened? Separation from heathen peoples was the first plank of the "sure covenant" so eagerly signed some few years before (see 10:30). What short memories the people of God sometimes possess! And what confirmation this is of the perpetual proneness of the human heart to wander from the ways of the Lord.

Cleansing the Temple (13:4-9)

But complete obedience to the Word of God in respect to separation from the Moabites and Ammonites (see v. 1) was not carried out, because with the permission of Eliashib the high priest, Tobiah *the Ammonite* (see 2:10) was living in the temple. This evil arrangement was made before Nehemiah's return to Jerusalem (see "before this" of v. 4 with vv. 6-7). Certainly, no such accommodation would have been made with Nehemiah on the scene, for as the previous chapters disclose, Tobiah the enemy kept his distance, opposing the rebuilding of Jerusalem by various indirect devices (see 2:10, 19; 4:3; 6:10-12, 17, 19).

In Nehemiah's absence, however, Tobiah was able to inveigle Eliashib the priest into providing him with living quarters in the temple by converting a large storage room for tithes and offerings into a splendidly furnished apartment (vv. 4-5). Thus, acting with all the subtlety of Satan, Tobiah was able to establish his central headquarters in this very strategic place and from there he purposed to continue his work against Nehemiah and the other spiritual leaders who tried to maintain the biblical lines of separation from evil.

Malachi's sharp words of censure against the priests (see Mal. 1:6—2:9) reveal that he at least did not hesitate to rebuke them openly for their low spiritual state leading to this and other glaring instances of laxity.

And then, unexpectedly no doubt, Nehemiah returned. Just as the golden calf was made in Moses' absence, an alien was installed in the temple during Nehemiah's absence. And when he learned the awful details (from Malachi?) he must have wept. The text reads, "And it grieved me sore" (v. 8), or more literally, "it was evil to me." With all the energy of his forceful personality and with deep, righteous indignation, he acted, personally throwing out of the temple chambers all of the household furniture of Tobiah. Did he then order it carried out of the city through the Dung Gate to be burned with the rest of the city refuse in the Hinnom Valley? It is not hard to imagine that it may have happened thus.

But Nehemiah was not finished. The temple chambers polluted by Tobiah had to be decontaminated (v. 9). Nehemiah gave the orders and there was immediate response on the part of the priests. Not even Eliashib raised a protest. He had more than met his match in Nehemiah. And when the washing, scouring, and sprinkling with blood were completed, the chambers were restored to their original use.

Nor should we be disturbed over Nehemiah's vigorous and decisive action, over his display of righteous indignation, for he was zealous for the house of God—it must not be defiled. In similar fashion the Lord cleansed the temple in His day, driving out the money changers who desecrated its precincts by their corrupt practices. Observes Cyril Barber:

Men of Nehemiah's ability are sorely needed today. Both in

the church and out of it we have long tolerated error. On the one hand there is false doctrine and a pseudopiety that allows the enemies of the truth to minimize the cardinal tenets of the faith and to control the curricula of our colleges and seminaries; on the other hand, the old principles of morality and integrity have been set aside for policies built upon expediency and the belief that the end justifies the means. These trends in both sacred and secular spheres need to be challenged by those who adhere to and practice the principles of godliness. But the cause of spiritual decline needs to be attacked at the root, where it began, in the toleration of evil" (*Nehemiah and the Dynamics of Effective Leadership*, p. 169).

Restoration of the Levites (13:10-14)

Nehemiah next discovered that the people were not bringing their tithes to the temple, a direct violation of another part of the "sure covenant" (see 10:35-39). Presumably, this is why a temple storage chamber was available for Tobiah; though it normally held foodstuffs for the support of the Levites, it had become empty. In order to escape starvation, the Levites had dispersed to the farm areas from which Nehemiah had brought them (see 12:28-29). The result was the crippling of the temple services.

Malachi had sternly addressed the people concerning this problem: "Will a man rob God? Yet ye have robbed Me. But ye say, 'Wherein have we robbed Thee?' In tithes and offerings. Ye are cursed with a curse: for Ye have robbed Me, even this whole nation. Bring ye all the tithes into the storehouse, that there may be meat in Mine house, and prove Me now herewith, saith the Lord of Hosts, if I will not open you the windows of heaven, and pour you out a blessing, that there shall not be room enough to receive it" (Mal. 3:8-10).

Apparently, the people did not respond to the prophet's appeal and so Nehemiah went directly to the rulers, reprimanding them for their negligence in this matter of the Law. Following this, he regathered the dispersed Levites and reestablished them in their places of responsibility in the temple.

The response of the people now appears to have been immediate. With the temple services again in operation, the tithes of

corn (grain), wine, and oil were brought to the storehouses
(v. 12). Reliable men were selected from among the Levites and
placed in charge of the storehouses and of the distribution of
goods to their fellow Levites (v. 13). Thus, a third critical abuse
was eliminated. But the task was not over and Nehemiah interrupted his report with his characteristic appeal, "Remember me,
O my God concerning this . . ." Far from being a self-seeking
and self-promoting leader, Nehemiah wanted only the providential
direction of God and His approval of his deeds. What a rare but
needed combination to be found in a Christian leader—courage,
decisiveness, and dependence on the Lord.

A visitor to the home of Gary Player, the champion pro golfer,
was struck by a plaque on the wall which read, "God loathes
mediocrity." He says, "If you're going to keep company with
Me, don't embarrass Me." (Ted W. Engstrom, *The Making of a
Christian Leader*, Grand Rapids: Zondervan Publishing House,
1976, p. 200).

In his life and service for God, Nehemiah was characterized
not by mediocrity, but by excellence, a worthy goal for every
Christian.

Enforcement of the Sabbath (13:15-22)

Nehemiah had further cause for alarm as he observed life in the
outlying provinces of Judah as well as in Jerusaem itself. In both
areas he was distressed to see evidence of Sabbath desecration. In
the towns and villages of Judah he saw Jews treading winepresses
on the Sabbath while others were loading their donkeys with all
kinds of products and bringing them to Jerusalem for the market
of the new week (v. 15). In addition, men from Tyre, probably
resident representatives of Tyrian fish companies, were actually
selling their salted and dried fish from the Mediterranean, raising
their raucous voices in the Jerusalem markets and disturbing the
peace and quiet of the Jewish Sabbath.

Of course, the fault lay with those Jews who labored in the
provinces and with those who bought Phoenician wares in Jerusalem on the Sabbath. Not only were the Jews violating their oath
(see 10:31) but they were also breaking the important fourth
commandment (see Ex. 20:8-11). And that was no small matter,
for the law of the Sabbath which set aside the seventh day for

Israel as one of complete rest was a memorial to God's rest after the six days of Creation and was instituted as a sign to the surrounding nations of Israel's special relationship to Jehovah (see Ezek. 20:12, 20).

Nehemiah went directly to the nobles who were governing the city and who bore responsibility for the profaning of the Sabbath (v. 17). He charged them to remember the lesson of history—perhaps he read to them from the scroll of Jeremiah the clear warning which their fathers had ignored to the ultimate sorrow of the nation (see Jer. 17:21-27). The closing words of Jeremiah's address to that former generation were somber: "But if ye will not hearken unto Me to hallow the Sabbath Day, and not to bear a burden, even entering in at the gates of Jerusalem on the Sabbath Day; then will I kindle a fire in the gates thereof, and it shall devour the palaces of Jerusalem, and it shall not be quenched." It happened as Jeremiah warned—and it could happen again, declared Nehemiah, if current Sabbath desecrations were not brought to an immediate halt (v. 18).

Apparently, the nobles were unmoved by Nehemiah's passionate appeal. He therefore took immediate charge of the situation, ordering the heavy main gates of Jerusalem closed from Friday evening to Saturday evening, posting some of his private servants at the gates to see that they remained closed on the Sabbath and that no one smuggled in merchandise (v. 19).

But the merchants did not return to their homes. They settled down outside the walls and set up their stalls there, tempting the townspeople to go out to them (v. 20). The LXX (Septuagint or Greek translation of the Old Testament) reads here, "And they all lodged and engaged in business outside of Jerusalem."

This devious behavior aroused Nehemiah's anger, and probably climbing to the top of the wall and shaking his fist at the merchants, he vigorously denounced them and warned that if they hung around on the outskirts of the walls again on the Sabbath he would personally attack them. The people were awed at the prospect of having to do battle with such a one-man army—and with good reason as the next paragraph reveals (see v. 25). Nehemiah records their response matter-of-factly, almost as a postscript, "From that time forth came they no more on the Sabbath" (v. 21).

With the passing of the crisis Nehemiah's servants, who had been ordered to watch the gates, were replaced by Levites for whom this duty was considered sacred. On their faithfulness, to some degree, would depend the nation's fidelity to the Sabbath (v. 22).

The record of this dramatic incident closes with Nehemiah's usual plea for remembrance. Whether this aggressive and dedicated leader was dealing with enemies foreign or domestic, whether he was involved in political, social, or religious issues, fellowship with God in prayer was always a top priority. It reminds us of Stonewall Jackson who said,

> I have so fixed the habit of my mind that I never raise a glass of water to my lips without asking God's blessing, never seal a letter without putting a word of prayer under the seal, never take a letter from the post without a brief sending of my thoughts heavenward, never change my class in the lecture room without a minute's petition for the cadets who go out and for those who come in.

Condemnation of Mixed Marriages (12: 23-31)

Nehemiah's work was not yet finished, for on a later tour of the remote frontiers of Judah he discovered to his great dismay that some of the Jews had married women of Ammon, Moab, and the Philistine city of Ashdod. Not only was this practice contrary to the Law of Moses (Ex. 34:15-16; Deut. 7:1-4), but it had been firmly dealt with just 30 years before by Ezra (see Ezra 9:1-4). More recently, the "sure covenant" had been signed affirming that intermarriage with the heathen would not be practiced, and a subsequent violation of that oath was dealt with in Jerusalem (see 13:1-4). The perennial problem must now be faced in the outlying districts. The situation was serious because the children of these mixed marriages could not even speak Hebrew, the language of the Jews (v. 24). How then could they be instructed in the Law at home or in the synagogue?

The New Testament adds its consistent witness against marriages between believers and unbelievers. Paul directed believers to marry "only in the Lord" (1 Cor. 7:39). Yet today as in previous ages, some believers rationalize that they will lead the unsaved mate to the Lord—but it rarely works that way and children more often than not follow the ways of the unregenerate parent.

Edith Schaeffer, cofounder of L'Abri, puts her finger on the root of such behavior then and now:

> The present atmosphere is like a smog that seems to creep in the door of the church when the organ is playing the wedding music and the roses are still fresh with the florist's dew. Voices seem to be chanting behind the music. 'Only do what you want to do—Don't do anything that is hard—Fight for your own rights, even if it means destroying everything—Put yourself first—Never mind what anyone else thinks—Pay the other person back—Get even—Do your own thing—Express yourself—Get fulfilled one way or another—Be free —Get rid of old mores and customs—Break out of the prison of social opinions—there are no lasting relationships possible, so walk out as soon as you feel like it—Nothing is worth working for—Be open-minded—Follow the crowd—Everything is relative, anyway!" (*What Is A Family?* [Old Tappan, New Jersey: Fleming H. Revell Co., 1975], pp. 31-32)

Nehemiah was well aware of the seriousness of this situation. Hearing these children speak in the languages of Israel's enemies, and knowing they could neither speak nor understand Hebrew, sent the governor's anger to a high pitch. He knew that when a family breaks down, a nation breaks down. Nehemiah recorded his reactions: "So I argued with these parents and cursed them and punched a few of them and knocked them around and pulled out their hair. . . ." (v. 25, LB). Showing his anger in this typical oriental fashion, it is clear Nehemiah meant business. It would appear that he forced the dissolving of those marriages as Ezra had (see v. 30a and Ezra 10:19). Determined to prevent recurrence of this practice, he made them swear that no more mixed marriages would be contracted (v. 25b).

In order to convince the Jews of the foreboding character of their sin, Nehemiah used the sad illustration of Solomon, a uniquely honored and divinely chosen king who nonetheless was caused to sin by the foreign women he married. The consequence of

Solomon's sin was the rending in two of the nation, a tragedy from which they had not recovered. And, Nehemiah asked, should the same sin that had brought God's judgment in a previous generation now be tolerated? (vv. 26-27)

Before concluding the report of this final act of reformation, special mention was made of the most outstanding offender who perhaps led many others to sin by his influence and example. The culprit was a grandson of Eliashib, the high priest. Apparently, during Nehemiah's absence this young man married the daughter of Sanballat, the governor of Samaria and hateful enemy of the Jews. This marriage was a flagrant offence because it formed a treasonable alliance with Israel's foe and compromised the purity of the high priesthood (see Lev. 21:6-8, 14-15). Nehemiah's response to this travesty was understandably drastic. He said simply, "Therefore I chased him from me" (v. 28c). Not wanting this violator anywhere around, he expelled him from the community, praying that God would remember those who had thus defiled the priesthood (v. 29). Malachi's scathing words to the priests (Mal. 2:1-8) form an excellent commentary on Nehemiah's petition. The prophet concluded, "But ye are departed out of the way; ye have caused many to stumble at the Law: ye have corrupted the covenant of Levi, saith the Lord of hosts."

Josephus (*Antiquities,* X1, 8, 2) though confusing the chronology, reports that when this young man, named Manasseh, was banished he fled to his father-in-law in Samaria with a copy of the Torah or Pentateuch, and established a rival worship on Mt. Gerizim (see John 4:20).

Concluding his moving narrative, Nehemiah summarized his achievements quite briefly. While he could have compiled an extensive list of his contributions, he modestly mentioned only his work of purification by which he purged the land of heathen wives and their pagan customs (v. 30a) and his work of organization by which he reinstated the priests and Levites in their assigned duties.

The old governor's final recorded words were, "Remember me, O my God, for good." The man who lived his entire life in God's presence, and who earnestly desired His approval on all his actions, pleaded to be remembered with blessing, not only for the short remainder of his days on earth, but also for the life to come.

Nehemiah's greatest desire was to experience David's hope, "Surely goodness and mercy shall follow me all the days of my life: and I will dwell in the house of the Lord forever" (Ps. 23:6).

The impact of Nehemiah on his own time can be measured by reading his memoirs. But what of his influence on future generations? Did the results of his work soon die out? Without question, Nehemiah, together with Ezra, made it possible for the true Jewish faith to survive in the dark centuries that followed. And survive it must because in the "fulness of time" God would send His Son, and there must be a remnant of believing ones who would be ready to welcome Him (Simeon and Anna, see Luke 2:25ff.). Howard Crosby said of Nehemiah, "We may believe that his influence ran down private channels in families and humble houses to the very time of the Messiah, making green lines of spiritual growth amid the arid desert of Judaism" (*The Book of Nehemiah*, 1877, p. 58).

Nehemiah's life and ministry still speak, for he is clearly set forth in Scripture as a model of capable, godly leadership. The principles he adopted and the methods he followed are just as effective today as in postexilic Jerusalem.

In these days when all areas of life are filled with confusion and are falling into disorder, we do well to subject our souls to the steadying, refreshing influence of a man like Nehemiah. His example will teach us to be specific in our purposes toward God and our church, to turn our wishbones into backbones, and to put feet and hands to our high-sounding resolutions" (*Bible Knowledge*, Oct.-Dec., 1968, p. 105).

It is well to note that Nehemiah was not a priest or a prophet. He was a layman who put himself as well as his gifts and abilities entirely at God's disposal. Who would doubt that when he entered the Lord's presence he heard the words, "Well done, thou good and faithful servant"? There can be no higher goal than that for any of us.